MINUTE GUIDE TO

SAP R/3

by Simon Sharpe

®

A Division of Macmillan Computer Publishing
201 West 103rd St., Indianapolis, Indiana 46290 USA

C000262168

I dedicate this book to Carol, who had faith in me even when I didn't myself.

©1997 by Que® Corporation

Library of Congress Catalog Card Number: 96-69616

International Standard Book Number: 0-7897-0898-1

99 98   8   7   6   5   4

Interpretation of the printing code: the rightmost double-digit number is the year of the book's first printing; the rightmost single-digit number is the number of the book's printing. For example, a printing code of 97-1 shows that this copy of the book was printed during the first printing of the book in 1997.

Screen reproductions in this book were created by means of the program Collage Plus from Inner Media, Inc., Hollis, NH.

Printed in the United States of America

Publisher Joe Wikert

Executive Editor Bryan Gambrel

Brand Director Greg Wiegand

Acquisitions Editor Martha O'Sullivan

Technical Editors Steve Davis and Rich Ward

Product Development Specialist John Gosney

Production Editors Audra Gable, Tom Lamoureux

Technical Specialist Nadeem Muhammed

Book Designer Barbara Kordesh

Cover Designer Dan Armstrong

Production Team Tricia Flodder, Mary Hunt, Daniela Raderstorf, Christy Wagner

Indexer Chris Wilcox

WE'D LIKE TO HEAR FROM YOU!

As part of our continuing effort to produce books of the highest possible quality, Que would like to hear your comments. To stay competitive, we *really* want you, as a computer book reader and user, to let us know what you like or dislike most about this book or other Que products.

You can mail comments, ideas, or suggestions for improving future editions to the address below, or send us a fax at (317) 581-4663. For the online inclined, the address of our Internet site is **http://www.mcp.com** (World Wide Web).

In addition to exploring our forum, please feel free to contact me personally to discuss your opinions of this book at **bgambrel@mcp.com**.

Thanks in advance—your comments will help us to continue publishing the best books available on computer topics in today's market.

Bryan Gambrel
Executive Editor
Macmillan Computer Publishing
201 West 103rd Street
Indianapolis, Indiana 46290
USA

CONTENTS

INTRODUCTION

SAP R/3 is an integrated business system designed to help organizations run such business processes as managing inventory, creating requisitions, processing sales orders, paying invoices, and so on. SAP R/3 covers a wide spectrum of business processes.

In the past, computer systems were specified and brought into organizations by each individual department: Human Resources chose its own system, Materials Management chose its system, Accounting chose its system, and so on.

Although each of those systems may have been the best choice for a particular department, keeping them working together was very expensive. Moreover, this kind of complex patchwork system inhibited change in organizations—and we all know what happens to organizations that can't change quickly.

SAP R/3 provides a single integrated system to handle the needs of all departments in a corporation. This integration is the single biggest advantage to moving to SAP R/3. Also, because SAP R/3 is a client-server–based system, its versatility is further enhanced.

 Client-Server In client-server computing, part of the processing runs on your desktop PC (the client), and part runs on central shared computers (servers). The presentation and pre-processing is done on your PC; the information is stored on servers.

SAP R/3 consists of a series of application areas. Figure I.1 shows those areas and how they interconnect.

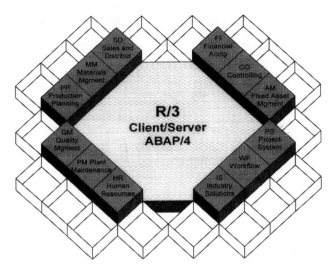

FIGURE I.1   The SAP R/3 system components.

WHO IS THE *10 MINUTE GUIDE TO SAP R/3* FOR?

This book is for anyone who fits one of these descriptions:

- You want to quickly learn how to get the most out of SAP R/3.

- You are new to SAP R/3.

- You have learned only one SAP R/3 method, and you are looking for new ways to save time.

- You want to become more self-sufficient so that you can find your own answers instead of calling your technical support team. (Because SAP R/3 is such a versatile product, each company can set it up in a different way. Therefore, you should look to your organization's support staff for job-specific training.)

Note to Corporate Trainers

This book is an ideal starting point for training your staff on SAP R/3. You can even set up your training system with data similar to that in the book's examples. The examples are all taken from MM, but the principles that are shown apply to all modules. The book can be used as an effective tool if you break it down in this way:

- Chapters 1–12 give a good grounding in the basics.

- Chapters 13–23 offer tips to make the users more productive.

- Appendixes A, B, and C offer a broad overview of all the modules.

How to Get the Most from This Book

Be aware that your screen might not match the examples in this book. The screen shots in this book come from a number of hypothetical and demo systems; your system may be configured differently. For example, your company may not be using the SAP R/3 MM Purchasing module that is used as an example in the book. However, you should be able to apply the concepts these lessons teach to other SAP R/3 modules.

Because SAP R/3 is so incredibly versatile, no two configurations will be the same. However, if you keep the following points in mind, you will be able to understand and use the information presented in this book and apply it to your own specific situation.

- Although SAP R/3 is accessible from a variety of desktop computers, this book is based on Windows. You will need basic Windows skills to understand this book.

- You will get the most from the book if you sit down and work through the examples on your system.

- Where concrete examples are essential in this book, they are drawn from the Materials Management area around *Purchase Requisitions*. This is because purchase requisitions (which are used to control material purchases) are basic, easily understood business documents.

- SAP R/3 provides you with excellent guidance and help facilities. In fact, new users are sometimes overwhelmed by the variety and amount of information that SAP R/3 can provide. This book will guide you through SAP R/3 and show you how to take advantage of the help SAP R/3 makes available to you.

Conventions and Icons Used in This Book

This book uses the following conventions to draw your attention to particular text (such as information you will see on-screen and information you will enter into the system).

On-screen text	On-screen information appears in bold type.
What you type	Information you type appears in bold blue type.
Items selected	Commands, options, and icons you select (or keys you press) appear in blue type.
Menu title, Menu command	When referring to menu commands, this book uses the format *menu title, menu command*. Therefore, the statement "choose File, Properties" means to "open the File menu and select the Properties command."

In addition to those conventions, the *10 Minute Guide to SAP R/3* uses the following icons to identify helpful information:

 Plain English icons mark new or unfamiliar terms that are defined in (you guessed it) "plain English."

Timesaver Tip icons say, "Look here for ideas that cut corners and confusion."

Panic Button icons identify common trouble areas for new users and offer practical solutions.

Finally, some lessons include a "What You Need for This Lesson" reminder. Be sure you meet the requirements listed there (which might include proper access to a particular screen or a previously created document) before you begin work on that respective lesson.

Acknowledgments

Thanks to Wayne Thrower from the SAP Toronto office. Without his help, this book would not have been possible. Thanks to Martha O'Sullivan for her patience and tireless efforts. Thanks to the whole team at Que for their guidance, advice, and suggestions. You people are real professionals. Thanks to the team in the SAP Calgary office for providing me access to their system and for their comments and suggestions.

Trademarks

All terms mentioned in this book that are known to be trademarks have been appropriately capitalized. Que cannot attest to the accuracy of this information. Use of a term in this book should not be regarded as affecting the validity of any trademark or service mark.

"SAP" is a registered trademark of SAP Aktiengesellschaft, Systems, Applications and Products in Data Processing, Neurottstrasse 16, 69190 Walldorf, Germany. The publisher gratefully acknowledges SAP's kind permission to use its trademark in this publication. SAP AG is not the publisher of this book and is not responsible for it under any aspect of press law.

ACCESSING SAP R/3

1

In this lesson, you will learn how to log on and off SAP R/3 and how to change your password.

 Say It Right SAP is pronounced "ESS AY PEE"; it's not like the sap in a tree.

WHAT YOU NEED BEFORE LOGGING ON

Before you can access SAP R/3 from your PC, you must satisfy a few preliminary requirements:

- You need to have the SAP R/3 *client software* (also called SAP GUI—Graphical User Interface) installed on your PC.

- You need to be connected to a *network* through which you can access your SAP R/3 server. You can usually arrange this through your local support organization.

- You need a user name and password to log on to SAP R/3. You can also arrange this through your local support organization.

- You need to know the client name of the system to which you want to connect.

 Client Software Programs on your PC that access information from an SAP R/3 *server computer* (a central computer that holds your SAP R/3 data files).

Network A collection of PCs connected together. You may also be able to dial in to your network by modem to access SAP R/3 remotely.

CLIENTS AND CLIENT NAMES

Many people misunderstand what the *client name* is. It is the name of the SAP R/3 system to which you are connecting.

Most companies have several clients designated for different tasks. For example, one hypothetical company has the following setup:

- The Client 401 Training system is used for training new users. Eventually, the training data is discarded. Purchase orders created here are not issued, and the customer orders are not filled. Therefore, this is a safe practice area.

- The Client 101 Production system is the live system used to run the business. It is not safe to practice here.

Using the Correct Client   Learn the name of your company's training system from your support organization and make sure you are connecting to the system you need. It is frustrating to find out the work you intended to save was actually entered into the training system. It can also be dangerous to practice on the Production system.

LOGGING ON

You can access SAP R/3 from a variety of different desktop computers and software. While the examples here are intended for Windows 95, access from other operating systems will be similar.

You start from the Windows desktop. The first step of the actual process will vary from company to company, but there will be either an icon on your desktop or an item on the Windows 95 Start menu.

- If there is an SAP R/3 icon on your Windows desktop, double-click it to launch SAP R/3.

- If there is no icon on the desktop, click the Start button, move through the menu, and click the SAP R/3 menu item to launch SAP R/3.

Either way, the SAP R/3 logon screen appears (see Figure 1.1). Notice the screen title SAP R/3. The screen title helps you keep track of where you are in SAP R/3.

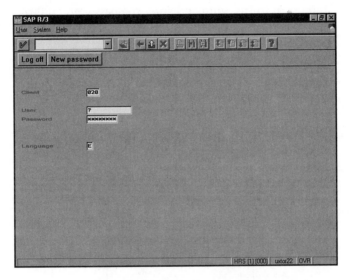

FIGURE 1.1 Type the client name, your user name, and your password to log on to SAP R/3.

Can't Find the Icon? Some companies use customized SAP R/3 startup programs, and some name the icons after the project that initiated SAP R/3. For example, the icon might be called RMIS if your company installed SAP R/3 with a project named Retail Marketing Information System. If you don't see an SAP R/3 icon or an item on the Start menu, the SAP R/3 client software may not be installed on your PC yet. Call your local support organization to get help.

Follow these steps to log on to SAP R/3 from the logon screen:

1. Enter the name of your company's training system in the Client field.

2. Press the Tab key to move to the User name field, and then enter the name you were given. This is usually an abbreviation or a number instead of your full name.

3. Tab down to Password and enter the password you were given. For security purposes, your password will not appear on-screen as you type it.

4. Depending on your company's setup, the Language field may or may not be filled in. If it is not, type E for English.

5. Press Enter to enter your information.

6. The first time you log on, the Password Change dialog box shown in Figure 1.2 appears, prompting you to change your password (for security reasons). Type your new password twice, making sure you type it the same way in both fields. Then click Confirm.

Figure 1.2   The Password Change dialog box.

7. Read the information in the SAP R/3 Copyright dialog box that appears, and then click Continue. The SAP R/3 home screen appears.

Figure 1.3 shows the main SAP R/3 screen. This is where you'll start all of your tasks and work. You'll learn about the elements that make up this screen in Lesson 2.

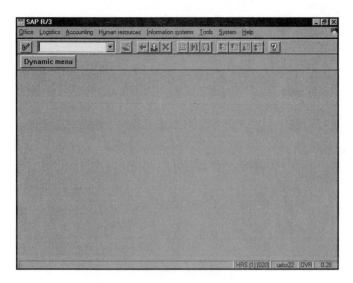

FIGURE 1.3   The SAP R/3 home screen.

PASSWORD PANIC

Remember these points about your passwords:

- Your user name and password authorize you to perform certain tasks. For example, if you are in Purchasing, your user name will probably allow you to perform only the tasks related to your Purchasing duties.

- Some companies set up SAP R/3 with almost universal display access. This means that any user can look at virtually every record, except those of a sensitive nature.

- You will be given either a special temporary user name for training or your permanent user name right away.

- Be careful when choosing a password. Don't write it down or use words or names that can be guessed easily. (Combinations of letters and numbers are more secure.)

- Your password must be between three and eight characters, and it cannot start with three of the same character.

LOGGING OFF

To log off from SAP R/3, do one of the following:

- Click the Close (X) button at the right end of the SAP R/3 title bar.

- Press and hold the Alt key and press the F4 key.

The Log Off confirmation box appears (see Figure 1.4). Click Yes to log off, or click No to cancel.

FIGURE 1.4 Do you really want to log off?

CHANGING YOUR PASSWORD

After the first time you log on, SAP R/3 will not present you with the dialog box to change your password. When you want to change your password again, go to the logon screen (shown in Figure 1.1). From there, follow these steps:

1. Enter the appropriate client name.

2. Enter your user name and your current password.

3. Click the New Password button. The password dialog box appears.

4. Enter your new password in both fields and click the Transfer button.

In this lesson, you learned how to log on and off SAP R/3, how to specify which Client system to connect to, and how to change your password. In the next lesson, you will learn the components of the SAP R/3 interface.

USING THE SAP R/3 INTERFACE

2

In this lesson, you will learn how to use the components of the SAP R/3 interface.

A LOOK AT THE SAP R/3 INTERFACE

As you learned in Lesson 1, when you launch SAP R/3, the SAP logon screen appears. Figure 2.1 shows the logon screen and points out the main elements of the user interface.

User Interface   The controls and displays you use to operate something. In your car, for example, the user interface would consist of the steering wheel, the pedals, and the dashboard.

The title bar in this figure reads **SAP R/3**. This changes according to which screen you are looking at. The title bar also can help you confirm that you are where you need to be.

The menu bar contains a number of menus from which you select commands to perform your tasks. Which menus are available changes depending on which screen you are on. Two selections that are available from all screens are System and Help. You'll learn more about menus in Lesson 3.

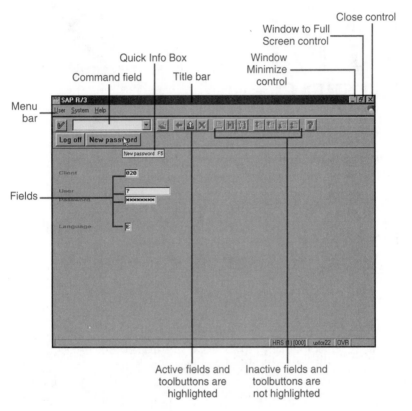

FIGURE 2.1 The SAP R/3 user interface.

Three standard Windows controls appear in the upper-right corner of the title bar:

- The **Window Minimize** control minimizes the SAP R/3 window to a button on your taskbar (where it remains active and you can get to it easily). You can bring it back to full-size by clicking it or by pressing Alt+Tab.

- The **Window to Full Screen** control changes your SAP R/3 session from occupying only a window on your screen to taking up the full screen. You might want to use this to check information in another system (to check your e-mail, for example) while using SAP R/3. When your session is occupying only a window, the window to full screen control is replaced with a maximize button, which you can click to make SAP R/3 take up the full window again.

- The **Close** control shuts down your SAP R/3 session (after you confirm that this is really what you want to do).

The toolbuttons across the top of the screen function as shortcuts you can use to perform common tasks. SAP R/3 displays active toolbuttons in color; shadowed toolbuttons do not apply to the active screen. (You'll learn more about the toolbuttons later in this lesson.)

The figure shows a Quick Info box labeled "New Password F5." These boxes appear when you position the mouse pointer over a button. This one, in particular, indicates that you're pointing to the New Password button, which performs the same function as the F5 key—both open the New Password dialog box.

SAP R/3 uses *fields* to accept and display information. Some things you should consider when dealing with fields include:

- The length of a field shows you how many characters you can type in that field.

- The cursor (a flashing line or block) shows the field that you are currently in (the active field); anything you type appears in this field.

- SAP R/3 generally shows a field name for each field on the screen.

- When SAP R/3 displays a question mark in a field, you must enter something into the field before you can go any further. In the logon screen shown in Figure 2.1, for example, a user name is required. If you try to go on without filling in all the required fields, SAP R/3 gives you an error message.

SAP R/3 AND DIALOG BOXES

Sometimes SAP R/3 uses *dialog boxes* to display or request information. When a dialog box appears on-screen, it becomes the active window, and its title bar is highlighted in blue.

 Dialog Box A box that SAP R/3 displays in order to communicate with you. Dialog boxes are smaller than the full SAP R/3 window.

Figure 2.2 shows the new password dialog box. Note that its title bar is highlighted, and the main screen's title bar is no longer highlighted to show that it's not active. This means that only the dialog box is active. You cannot access anything on the main screen behind it until you have dealt with the dialog box. You must click the Cancel button or the Confirm button to close this dialog box and return to the main screen.

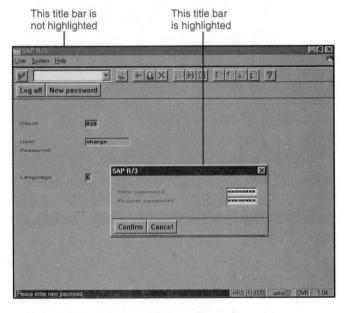

FIGURE 2.2   Only the dialog box is active.

Sometimes SAP R/3 presents you with several layers of dialog boxes. You must deal with those boxes in order to get back to your original screen.

The SAP R/3 Toolbar

The SAP R/3 toolbar is the row of toolbuttons across the top of the screen. Some buttons apply to all screens; others apply only to some screens. SAP R/3 tells you which are active by showing them in color. Shadowed toolbuttons do not apply to the screen displayed. Table 2.1 shows you the toolbuttons and describes each one.

TABLE 2.1   SAP R/3 Toolbuttons

Toolbutton	Name	Description
	Check	Functions the same as the Enter key. When you click this, SAP R/3 checks the values on the screen. If all values are okay, you move to the next screen. If values are not acceptable, you get an error message.
	Save/Post	Saves the current record you are working with and backs out to the previous screen. SAP R/3 highlights any missing data when you click this button.
	Back	Backs you out to previous screen.
	Exit	Backs you out to previous level.
	Cancel	Aborts a process and discards the information.

continues

TABLE 2.1   CONTINUED

TOOLBUTTON	NAME	DESCRIPTION
	Print	Prints the current document.
	Find	Finds specified text or numbers.
	Find Again	Finds the next occurrence of the specified text or numbers.
		Scrolls to the top of the screen.
		Scrolls up one screen.
		Scrolls down one screen.
		Scrolls to the bottom of the screen.
	Field Level Help	Tells you how SAP R/3 uses this field.

TIP   **Back and Exit**   If you are at the first screen in a series, the Back and Exit buttons will do the same thing. If you are at the third screen in a process, Back takes you back to the second screen, and Exit takes you right out of the process.

THE STATUS BAR

The *status bar* is usually displayed at the bottom of the SAP R/3 screen (see Figure 2.3). If your screen does not show the status bar, go to Lesson 19 "Customizing Your User ID" to learn how to turn it on.

SAP R/3 uses the status bar to pass along information. In particular, the message area part of the status bar contains a message preceded by one of the following codes:

Code	Meaning
W	Warning
E	Error
A	Abnormal End
I	Information

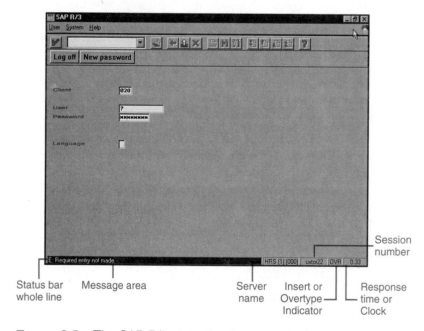

Figure 2.3   The SAP R/3 status bar keeps you informed.

In the case of Figure 2.3, the status bar message **E:Required Entry not made** is an error notice telling you that you need to fill in a field before you can proceed.

Status Bar Error Messages   New users sometimes do not notice error messages on the status bar, and they don't know why they are unable to go on. The first thing you should look at when you have a problem is the status bar.

On the right end of the status bar, you'll find the following information:

- **Server name**   This is different from the one you typed in to gain access to the system, which may seem a little awkward at first. In the case of Figure 2.3, the name is HRS(1) (020); HRS is the name of a demonstration system in the SAP Calgary office. We used the client code of 020 to access this system in Figure 1.1.

- **Session number**   You can have more than one SAP R/3 session open at once. See Lesson 18, "Using Transaction Codes" for details.

- **Insert/overtype indicator**   This indicates which typing mode you are in. You switch between insert and overtype modes when you press the Insert key.

- **Clock**   SAP R/3 provides a clock in the lower right corner. (You can also use this area to display the system response time. See Lesson 19, "Customizing Your User ID," for details.)

In this lesson, you learned the basics of the SAP R/3 user interface. In the next lesson, you will learn how to use the SAP R/3 screen elements to move between screens.

GETTING AROUND THE SCREEN

*In this lesson, you will learn how to get around the
SAP R/3 screen and how to get help on the fields displayed.*

USER REQUIREMENTS FOR THIS LESSON

To understand the examples in this lesson, you will need either:

- A user logon name with authority to create a purchase requisition.

- An *application area* where you have authority to create another *document*.

Application Area An area in SAP such as Purchasing, Human Resources, Plant Maintenance, and so on.

Document The generic name for a standard business form. Although you may be used to thinking of a document as paper, in this sense it refers to an electronic business transaction record. A Purchase Order is a document, as are a Maintenance Request and an Invoice.

The example used in this lesson is a purchase requisition, which is typical of many other business documents. If your user name does not give you the authority to create a purchase requisition, find out what it does have permission to create and use that document as your example.

Unauthorized Documents   It doesn't do any harm to try to create a document that your user name is not authorized for. You will, however, get an error message on the status bar.

GETTING TO AN SAP R/3 DOCUMENT ENTRY SCREEN

All business transactions involve documents. Sometimes documents are created automatically by SAP R/3, but at other times you will need to create documents yourself with a document entry screen. Document entry screens exist in all modules.

No matter what kind of document you want to create, you begin at the SAP R/3 home screen (refer to Figure 1.3 for a refresher). To access the purchase requisition document entry screen, follow these steps:

   1. Pull down the Logistics menu and choose Materials Management (see Figure 3.1). Notice that some commands have a small arrow beside them, which means that choosing the command will make a submenu appear, displaying more choices.

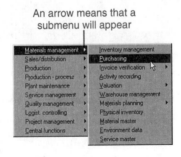

An arrow means that a submenu will appear

FIGURE 3.1   Going to Purchasing.

2. Choose Purchasing, and the Purchasing screen appears.

3. From the Purchasing screen, choose Requisition, Create. The Create Purchase Requisition: Initial Screen (shown in Figure 3.2) appears.

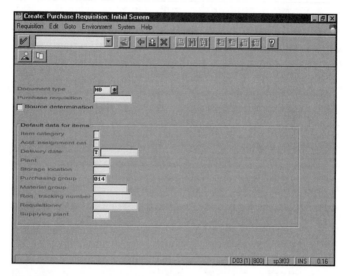

FIGURE 3.2   You're ready to create a purchase requisition.

 It Doesn't Look Like That   In this installation, some of the fields were "carried in." Depending on the installation, you could have different fields carried in.

4. Notice the little box to the left of "Source determination." This is called a selection box because a dot indicates that the function is turned on; a blank box indicates that the function is turned off. For this kind of document (purchase requisition), you can choose whether you want SAP R/3 to automatically determine the source of the material or not. For now, leave this box unchecked. Press Enter, and the document entry screen appears.

> **Two New Buttons** The buttons that show mountains and pages (in the upper-left corner) vary from screen to screen. To see what they do, point to them. In this case, they are "Item Overview" and "Copy Reference."

Figure 3.3 shows the Create Purchase Requisition: Item Overview screen. It is typical of the many document entry screens in SAP R/3.

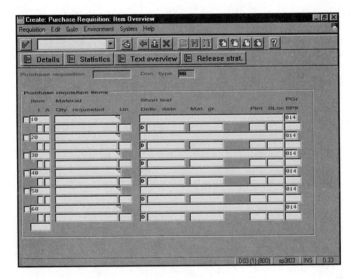

FIGURE 3.3 The purchase requisition document entry screen.

Many business documents have a single *header* and multiple *line items*. You can use this screen to enter a purchase requisition with one or more line items. You could request several kinds of product on a single purchase requisition. Each product would be listed as a single line item.

> **Line Item** One or more items that are part of a larger single document.
>
> **Header** Information that is common to all line items.

On a cash register receipt, the header contains the date, store, and so on. The line items designate the item's place among items, prices, and quantities.

In Figure 3.3, you can see the Purchase requisition and Doc. type header lines at the top. Because you have not yet created a requisition, the Purchase Requisition field is currently blank.

Also note the following things in Figure 3.3:

- The fields for each line item are *stacked* (there are two screen lines to contain each line item). The titles are stacked above the two lines in a pattern similar to the stacking fields themselves.

- There are selection boxes to the left of each line item. You will use these later to select a particular line item to work with.

- Because of the way the fields are stacked, some of the titles displayed are very short (like the A field). See the section "How the Fields Are Used" (later in this lesson) to learn how to get more details about any field.

 Don't Want Them Stacked?   SAP R/3 can display the fields two different ways. Choose Edit, Change Display to switch between the two formats.

GETTING AROUND AN SAP R/3 DOCUMENT ENTRY SCREEN

You can move around a document entry screen using any of the following methods:

- Press the Tab key and see how the cursor moves from field to field. Press and hold Shift and then press the Tab key, and you move back through the fields.

- You can move to any specific field by pointing to it and clicking.

- Within a field, use the cursor left and right keys to move around in the text you create.

- While typing in a field, you can use the Backspace or Delete key to remove characters. Backspace removes the character to the left of your cursor; Delete removes the one to its right.

OTHER WAYS OF GETTING AROUND

You can also use Function keys on SAP R/3 screens. You don't *need* to learn these keys because all of the functions are available with the mouse. However, experienced users sometimes find it more convenient to use the function keys.

To get a list of active function keys for a screen, press Ctrl+F (press and hold Ctrl and press F). SAP R/3 displays the list of function keys shown in Figure 3.4.

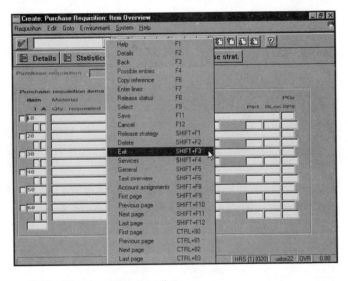

FIGURE 3.4   The function key list.

You can also call up this list by clicking the right mouse button anywhere on the SAP R/3 screen. (The list that appears varies from screen to screen, depending on what functions are available.) Click an item in the list to select it.

Keyboard Convenience If you are using a laptop and you don't want to bother with the mouse, you can use SAP R/3 from the keyboard. Activate the menus by pressing F10, use the cursor keys to highlight your selection, and then press Enter.

How the Fields Are Used

Move the cursor to the Material field and click the Field Level Help button on the toolbar. (See Lesson 2 for information on toolbar buttons.) SAP R/3 displays a dialog box that tells you how to use the Material field (see Figure 3.5).

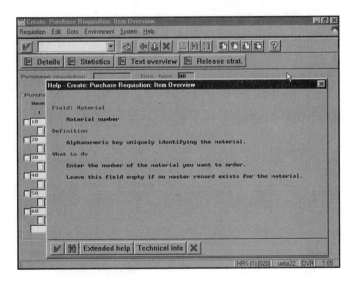

Figure 3.5   Field level help.

Sometimes SAP R/3 uses fields in different ways for different kinds of records. For the purchase requisition, in the material field, for example, you could be buying a material that your company commonly buys. In this case, somebody in your company may already have created a *master record* for this material. For a material that already exists on your system, you would enter a material number. For a one-time purchase of a material, you would leave the material field blank.

 Master Record Examples of master records are lists of products (material master) and lists of customers (customer master). (The dialog box in Figure 3.6 tells you to leave this field blank if the item you are buying is not listed in your material master file.)

Sometimes a term displayed in the field level help dialog box is highlighted. You can click a highlighted word to get a definition of it. Click the highlighted word material. Figure 3.6 shows the definition box that appears.

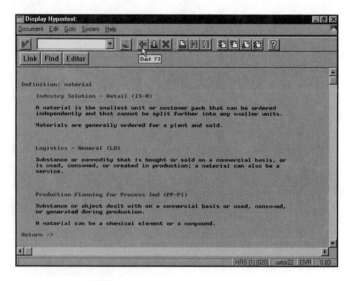

FIGURE 3.6 A definition box.

When you finish reading the definition, click Back to clear the definition box. To exit the field level help dialog box, click Cancel.

In this lesson, you learned how to get around on an SAP R/3 screen and how to get help with fields and definitions. In the next lesson, you will learn how to move between SAP R/3 screens.

MOVING BETWEEN SCREENS

*In this lesson, you will learn how to scroll around
on an SAP R/3 screen and how to move between screens. You will
also learn about the menus that are available on various screens.*

USER REQUIREMENTS FOR THIS LESSON

To work through this lesson, you will need one of the following:

- A user logon name with authority to create a purchase requisition

- An application area where you have authority to create another document

THE DIFFERENCE BETWEEN BACK AND EXIT

The Back button (the arrow pointing left), and the Exit button (the arrow pointing up) both move you back through your work to a screen you viewed earlier. Work through the following steps to learn firsthand the difference between the two.

1. As you learned in the last lesson, go to the Create Purchase Requisition: Item Overview screen.

2. Click the Back toolbar button. You are returned to the Create Purchase Requisition: Initial Screen. Note that you have not left the process of creating a Purchase Requisition, you have just *backed up* to an earlier screen.

3. Press Enter to go forward to the overview screen again.

4. Now, from the overview screen, click the Exit button. The first purchasing screen appears. In this case, you have *exited* the process of creating a Purchase Requisition.

5. Click Exit as many times as necessary until you get to the starting SAP R/3 screen. If you go too far, SAP R/3 displays a dialog box asking if you want to log off (see Figure 4.1).

 If You Get Lost... You can always get back to the initial SAP R/3 screen. Simply click the Exit button several times, and—no matter what—you can get back to a place you know.

Figure 4.1 If you press Exit enough times, you can log off.

6. In the Log Off dialog box, click Yes to log off, or click No to cancel the Exit command. (For our purposes, click No.)

 TIP **Close Button** You can log off SAP R/3 from any screen by clicking the Close (X) button.

Screen Buttons and Scroll Bars

To learn about screen buttons and toolbars, you can go into Release notes. (You don't really need to know anything about the release notes themselves—but they provide a convenient example that all users have access to.) Follow these steps:

1. From the initial SAP R/3 screen, select Help, Release
   Notes. The Find Release Notes screen appears. Note that it
   has three screen buttons: Complete List, Key word search,
   and Attributes.

 Screen Buttons The buttons that appear in the row
below the toolbar. You can click any of these buttons to
get to another screen or to launch other processing. The
screen buttons vary from screen to screen (unlike the
toolbar buttons, which stay the same all the time).

2. Click the Complete list button, and the Read Structure:
   Complete List of Release Notes Available screen appears
   (see Figure 4.2).

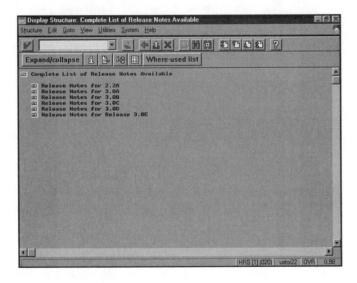

Figure 4.2   The Read Structure screen is like a table of contents
to a much larger document.

3. Click the plus sign (+) beside Release Notes for 3.0D to "open up" that topic. (Clicking the plus sign displays a topic's subtopics. Clicking the minus sign closes the topic again.)

4. Keep clicking plus buttons until you get to a screen that looks like the one in Figure 4.3.

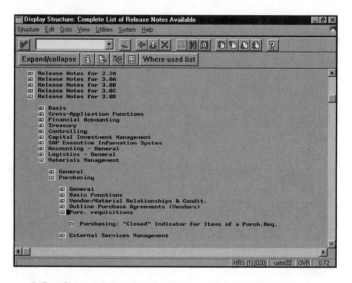

FIGURE 4.3   Several levels of a list.

5. The titles that don't have a plus or minus sign have no subtopics. Double-click an individual topic to read its text. Figure 4.4 shows an individual topic.

Notice the scroll bars that appear along the bottom and right sides of this screen. They are designed to make navigation of a large document easier. Read on to learn how to use the scroll bars.

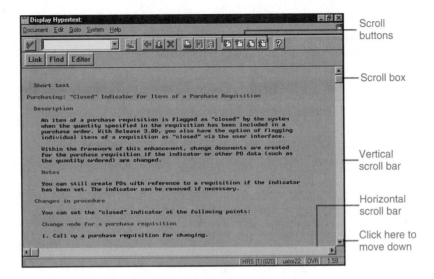

FIGURE 4.4   Open a topic and read the information on it.

SCROLLING AROUND A SCREEN

Sometimes, the text to be displayed is wider (or higher) than your screen. Sometimes it is both. You can use several tools to scroll around in your document.

When the list is longer than your screen, use these methods to move down (and do the opposite to move up):

- Move down a full page by pressing the Page Down key on the keyboard.

- Move down a full page (or to beginning or end) by clicking the scroll buttons on the toolbar.

- Move down a full page by clicking in the scroll bar below the scroll box.

- Move large amounts by dragging the scroll box downward (press and hold the mouse button, and then move the mouse). When you release the mouse button, the screen display moves down.

- Move down one line at a time by clicking the down arrow that appears at the bottom of the scroll bar.

When the document is wider than your screen, you can use the horizontal scroll bar in a similar way to scroll left and right.

No More Scrolling   When you can't move your scroll box down any further, you know you're at the bottom of the document.

Whereas scrolling allows you to move around within a document, menus allow you to move between screens.

Understanding the Menus

You learned in Lesson 2 that the menu bar is the line just below the title bar in the SAP R/3 screen. The following three menus exist on every screen for your convenience:

- **System**   This menu gives you access to system functions.

- **Help**   SAP R/3 makes plenty of clearly-written Help screens available online. Lessons 5 and 6 cover basic and advanced online help.

- It is easy to miss the user options menu, which is marked only by a colored logo at the far right of the menu bar. This menu controls your user id and is covered in more detail in Lesson 19.

Figure 4.5 shows each of these menus and the commands they contain.

FIGURE 4.5   These menus are always accessible.

SAP R/3 provides several other menus. As you may have noticed, however, the other menus in the menu bar change according to the task you're performing. Those menus include:

- **Object**   This is usually named after the kind of document you are creating. In this case, it's the Requisition menu.

- **Edit**   This has commands for things you can do to the current object (such as Copy, Paste, or Select).

- **Goto**   Several screens are usually associated with each object. The goto menu gives you one way to move between those related screens. In addition, commands on this menu are often duplicated on the screen buttons—which gives you two ways to get there.

- **Details**   Sometimes an object's main screen contains all of the commonly used fields, while less commonly used fields appear on different screens. The Details menu takes you to these screens.

- **Environment**   This menu allows you to work with other data associated with the current object.

- **View**   This menu allows you to select one of several views of your data.

Figure 4.6 shows each of the open menus. Take a good look at which commands are located on which menus. The submenus will also vary with the task you are doing.

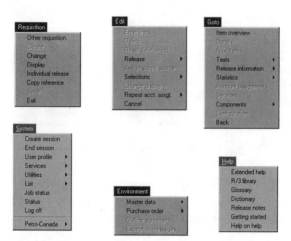

FIGURE 4.6   These menus change from screen to screen, with the exception of the Help and System menus.

 TIP   **Shadowed Selections**   An option that is shadowed is not currently available. For example, you can't save a record if there's no data in it, so the Save option might be shadowed.

 TIP   **You have Different Options?**   Like most everything about SAP, the menus are configurable so that any company can add custom functions to any menu.

In this lesson, you learned how to move from screen to screen and how to use screen buttons, scroll bars, and multilevel lists. In the next lesson, you will learn how to use the extensive Help facilities that SAP R/3 provides.

USING BASIC HELP

In this lesson, you will learn how to find the kind of help that applies to all SAP R/3 modules.

ONLINE HELP IN SAP R/3

SAP R/3 provides two kinds of online help: Basic Help (which you'll learn about in this lesson) and Task-Level Help (which is covered in Lesson 6). Learning how to make the most of both types of help will move you much closer to being a self-sufficient SAP R/3 user.

 Online Help   Manuals and help systems that are distributed and accessed electronically instead of on paper.

WHERE TO START WITH HELP

The first help you should look at is the basic help that "Getting started" provides. While you are learning to use SAP R/3, you may need to check this kind of help from time to time to remind you how to use parts of the SAP R/3 user-interface.

1. From the SAP R/3 screen, select Help, Getting Started. SAP R/3 displays the first help screen, which is shown in Figure 5.1. (The Help menu is available from any screen in SAP R/3.)

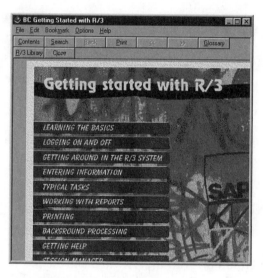

FIGURE 5.1   The first Basic Help screen.

2. Click Learning the Basics, and SAP R/3 displays the help
   screen shown in Figure 5.2.

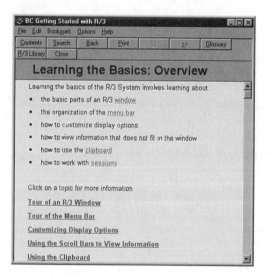

FIGURE 5.2   Dotted underlines point to more information.

3. Notice that some of the words have dotted underlines. This tells you that SAP R/3 can display information panels on these terms. To see an information panel, click the desired underlined text. For example, click menu bar, and SAP R/3 displays the pop-up panel shown in Figure 5.3.

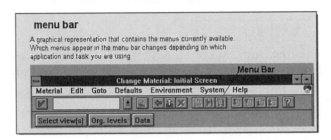

FIGURE 5.3   An information panel.

4. Click anywhere on the screen to get rid of the information panel and return to the first Basic Help screen.

5. Next, click Tour of an R/3 Window. Then click the window maximize control to get the big picture on help. The help screen expands to fill your screen (see Figure 5.4).

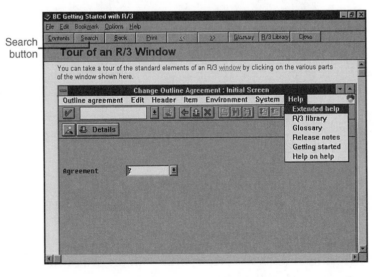

FIGURE 5.4   Getting a bigger view: a handy reference to the screen components.

Check It Out Try clicking a few of SAP R/3's icons inside the help screen. When you do, SAP R/3 gives you more details on the selected device.

THE TOPIC INDEX

Sometimes the help you need is not listed in the table of contents, like "Tour of an R/3 Window" was. When you run into such a case, you can use the index to locate those unlisted topics.

1. From any help screen, click the Search button below the menu bar to get to the topic index. Figure 5.5 shows the topic index.

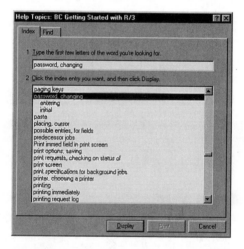

FIGURE 5.5 Using the index.

2. Either scroll down the list to find the topic you want, or start typing the topic (as shown in Figure 5.5) to cause the list to scroll down to the entry you are looking for.

3. Double-click the topic you want, such as password, changing, and SAP R/3 presents you with the details on that topic (see Figure 5.6).

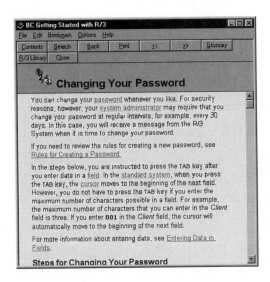

FIGURE 5.6   Zoom right in to the desired topic.

THE HIGH POWER SEARCH

The previous search method works well for finding details about subjects that are included in the index. However, there may be times when you can't find what you need using the topic index.

Windows 95 has a very powerful text search feature that works on SAP R/3 help files (and other software's help files). This feature helps you find help topics where the text itself contains words you are looking for.

TIP   **Searching Help Files**   This kind of search can help you with any Windows 95-based Help files.

To use the search feature, follow these steps:

1. Go back to the screen you saw in Figure 5.5 by clicking the Search button.

2. This time, click the Find tab instead of the Index tab. Windows displays the information dialog box shown in Figure 5.7.

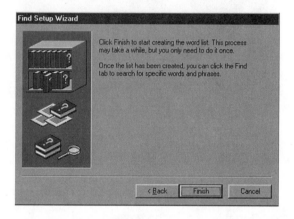

FIGURE 5.7 Windows is preparing to build a little database.

3. The first time you use Topic search, Windows quickly reads through the whole topic to build a list of words. Accept the recommended settings in the dialog box by clicking Next. Then click Finish in the displayed dialog box. (This process should take less than minute, during which time an animated display assures you that the process is still working.)

4. When Windows 95 finishes building its word list, enter the word you want to search for. For example, to find out how to get help regarding messages SAP R/3 is giving you, type the word **help**. SAP R/3 searches for the word and tells you that—in the present example—38 topics contain the word "help" (see Figure 5.8).

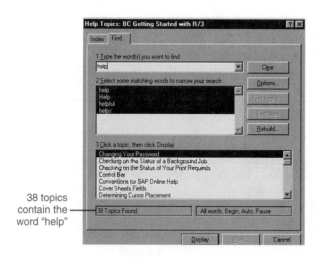

38 topics
contain the
word "help"

FIGURE 5.8   The High Powered find.

5. To narrow your search so that you don't have to look through all 38 matching entries, type a space after "help" and add the word **message**. SAP R/3 searches for messages that contain both the word "help" and the word "message," and then it reduces the number of topics found.

6. Click the topic you want to see—Getting help on messages, for our example—and click Display. Windows displays the specified topic as shown in Figure 5.9.

TIP   **This Is Important Information!** To get help on any error or warning message that SAP displays in the message area, click the message and click the Field Level Help toolbutton (the question mark).

You can use this same kind of text-searching in the task-level help system, which you will learn about in Lesson 6.

Global Searches and Subtopics Because SAP R/3 is so large, the help files are broken into smaller topics. This means that you cannot globally search all the help files using, for example, the words "purchase" and "requisition." (You would need to use the Materials Management help files for that type of task.)

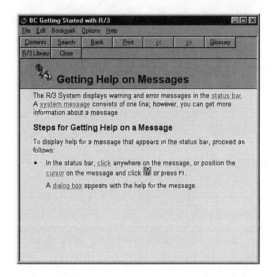

FIGURE 5.9 SAP R/3 finds the information you requested.

In this lesson, you learned how to use SAP R/3's Basic Help and how to access the information panels available. In the next lesson, you will learn how to use task-level help.

Using Task-Level Help

In this lesson, you will learn how to find specific detailed help on tasks you need to perform in SAP R/3. You will also learn to use context-sensitive help and to search the SAP R/3 Help Library for yourself.

WHAT YOU NEED FOR THIS LESSON

To practice using context-sensitive help, you need one of the following:

- A user name with the authority to get into the purchase requisition screen.

- Authority to get into another document-creation screen so that you can follow along.

WHAT TASK-LEVEL HELP CAN DO FOR YOU

SAP R/3 provides detailed step-by-step instructions on how to complete *all* tasks (such as creating a Purchase Requisition or changing a Work Order). Because SAP R/3 is a generic product used in different ways by different businesses, the detailed help it provides is also generic and covers features that you may never need to use where you work.

Company-Specific Instructions   If your organization provides guides on how to perform certain tasks on SAP R/3, those guides will probably be more specific than the SAP R/3 help system.

GETTING TO THE RIGHT HELP MODULE

You can get to the help module you need in two ways:

- Using the *context-sensitive* help
- Finding your own way in through the R/3 Library

Context-Sensitive Help   In this type of help system, the kind of help screen SAP R/3 shows you depends on which screen you are on when you ask for help.

GETTING IN BY CONTEXT

For this lesson, assume that you are looking for help related to creating a Purchase Requisition. To access context-sensitive help, start on the Create Purchase Requisition: Initial Screen. (If you don't remember how to get there, refer to Lesson 3.) From that screen, choose Help, Extended Help.

SAP R/3 checks to see which screen you are on and takes you into the appropriate help module. In this case, because you're on a Create Purchase Requisition screen, SAP displays help information on maintaining requisitions (see Figure 6.1).

Extended Help   This menu option is available no matter where you are in SAP R/3. The information it provides is different depending on where you are.

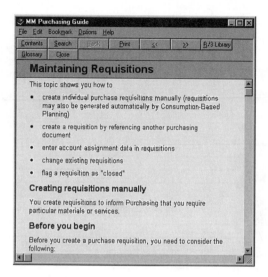

FIGURE 6.1   A task-specific help topic.

GETTING IN THROUGH THE R/3 LIBRARY

Context-sensitive help works well if you know how to get to the screen for which you need help. If you aren't sure even where to start, you will need to find your own way in through the SAP R/3 Help Library. The following steps walk you through doing just that.

1. From any SAP R/3 screen, choose Help, R/3 Library. SAP R/3 displays the Library Manager screen shown in Figure 6.2. Take a few moments to look at the options. The information here is word-for-word the same as the printed manuals that you can order from SAP.

TIP

Library Manager   This library contains an amazing amount of useful, well-written information. Because it is online, it's easy to search, and you don't have to bother trying to keep it up-to-date like you do paper manuals.

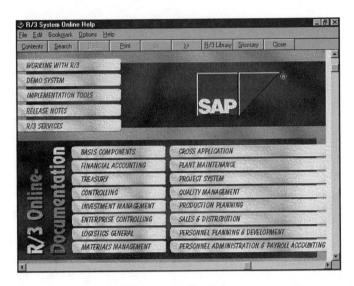

FIGURE 6.2 The SAP R/3 Library Manager.

2. To find help on creating a Purchase Requisition, click Materials Management. SAP R/3 displays the Materials Management help screen shown in Figure 6.3.

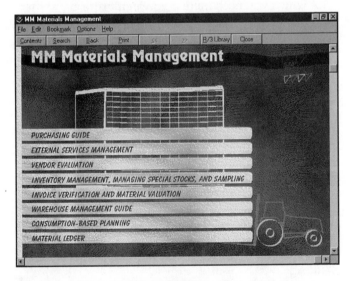

FIGURE 6.3 An index to Materials Management topics.

3. If the Help dialog box is not full-screen size, click the Window Maximize control to expand the Materials Management topic index to fill the screen.

4. Click the topic Purchasing Guide, and a more detailed help screen appears (see Figure 6.4).

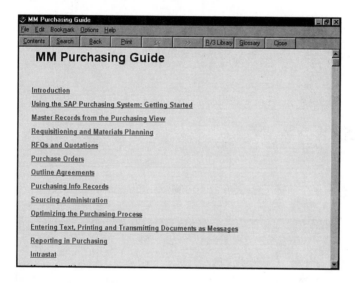

FIGURE 6.4   Click Requisitioning and Materials Planning to get down to even more detail.

5. Click Requisitioning and Materials Planning to get even more detailed information (see Figure 6.5).

General Topics   Don't underestimate the value of such general topics as About Requisitions. Topics like this give you background information that will help you understand the way work flows through the system. (These topics are not easy to find unless you enter the Help system through the Library Manager.)

6. Click Maintaining Requisitions, and the screen shown in Figure 6.6 appears. Does it look familiar? It should. It's the same screen you saw for context-sensitive help in Figure 6.1. The Help Library and the context-sensitive helps are just different paths to the same help files.

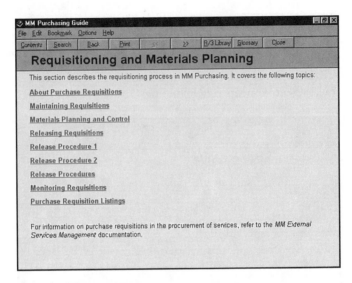

FIGURE 6.5 Requisitioning and Materials Planning.

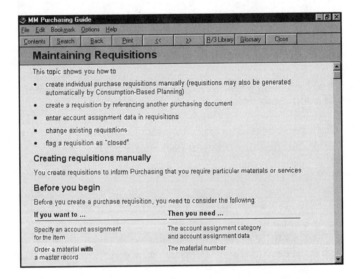

FIGURE 6.6 The Maintaining Requisitions help screen.

7. Use the scroll bar to move down through the topic until you find the information you need. Figure 6.7 shows just how detailed the help system is.

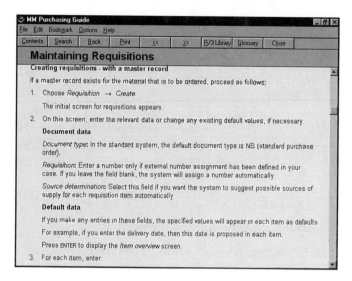

FIGURE 6.7   Step-by-step instructions exist for all tasks.

The point of this exercise was to show you that SAP R/3 provides a wealth of online help that you should dip into whenever you need to. If you use only the context-sensitive help, you may not see some of the other useful topics available in the SAP R/3 Help Library (like the general topics).

ONE CATCH

You may recall from Lesson 5 that you can search for help using the index and the full-text find function of Windows' help. You can use those methods on these modules, too, but because the SAP R/3 help is broken into smaller modules, you cannot globally search across the modules. You must be in the right module to find the help you need. For example, to find help on purchase requisitions, you must be in the Purchasing help module.

In this lesson you learned how to get step-by-step help on specific business processes. You also learned how to take advantage of context-sensitive help and the SAP R/3 Help Library. In the next lesson, you will learn how to create a business document.

7 LESSON

CREATING A DOCUMENT

In this lesson, you will learn how to create a business document, relying on SAP R/3 to help you through the process.

USER REQUIREMENTS FOR THIS LESSON

For this lesson, you need one of the following:

- A user logon name with authority to create a purchase requisition
- An application area where you have the authority to create a document, so that you can follow along

For the examples in this lesson, we will use a purchase requisition as our sample document. It is typical of other documents you create on SAP R/3.

To create this requisition, you need to know:

- A valid material number in your organization
- A valid material group in your organization
- The default date format for your User ID
- A valid plant code to deliver the material to

CREATING THE PURCHASE REQUISITION

1. From the SAP R/3 screen, choose Logistics, Materials Management, Purchasing. The Purchasing screen appears.

2. Choose Requisition, Create, and the Create Purchase Requisition: Initial Screen appears. (You first saw this screen in Lesson 3, Figure 3.2.)

3. Press Enter. If your company's configuration doesn't include a required entry for requisition number, the Create Purchase Requisition: Item Overview screen appears (see Figure 7.1). If you press Enter on a screen where values are required, SAP R/3 prompts you for the missing values.

 Required Entries As a rule, unless the field has a question mark in it, it is not a required entry. However, you will see exceptions to this later in this lesson.

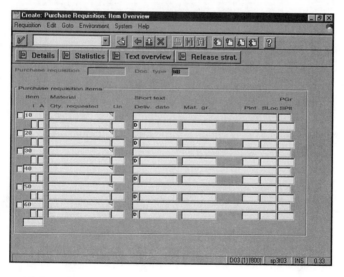

FIGURE 7.1 When you create a purchase requisition, you must specify the items to be requested.

4. To see how SAP R/3 uses the status line to communicate, click Save. SAP R/3 displays an error message in the status bar and temporarily shades all the fields to indicate that you cannot enter information in them (see Figure 7.2).

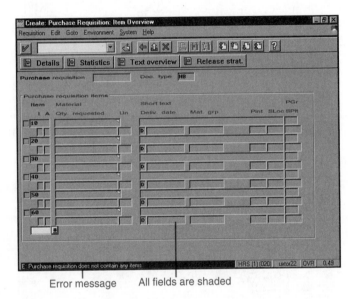

Error message   All fields are shaded

FIGURE 7.2   SAP R/3's status line says you are trying to save a requisition with no items on it.

5. Press the Esc key to acknowledge the message and to clear the fields. (Remember that to get more detail on an error message, you can click the message and click the Field Level Help toolbutton.)

Default Item Numbers   You don't need to enter the item number, it is assigned by SAP R/3. It is used to distinguish this item from others on the requisition. It may increase by ones or tens, depending on your system.

Field Level Help   Remember that if you need more information on a particular field, you can access Field Level Help from any screen.

6. Move your cursor to the first Material field and enter a valid material number for your company. Tab to the Plant (Plnt) field, enter the number of a plant that stocks the item, and press Enter. For the configuration shown in Figure 7.3, 1500–520 is the number for 10-W-30 motor oil. SAP R/3 looks up the number you typed to verify that it is a valid material number.

Code Entries   SAP R/3 represents many items with codes (product numbers, storage locations, and so on). If you enter a code that is not valid, SAP R/3 displays an error message on the status bar. If the code is valid, SAP R/3 looks up the description and inserts it into the Short text field. It also fills in the appropriate Un (Unit of Measure) and Mat. Gr. (Material Group), such as CSE (case) and 010 in Figure 7.3.

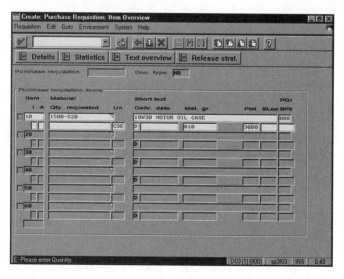

FIGURE 7.3   You type the material number, SAP R/3 looks up the rest.

7. Once a valid number has been entered, the cursor moves to the next required field that is empty. In the example shown, it is Quantity (Qty. Requested). The command line asks you how much of the item you want.

LET SAP R/3 LEAD THE WAY

If you aren't sure if you have filled in enough information to complete the record, you can let SAP R/3's "guiding light" help you along. Starting where you left off in the previous exercise, work through these steps to see an example of how SAP guides you through a task.

1. Enter a Purchasing Group (if you haven't already) and press Enter. SAP R/3 looks at the fields and displays a message like the one in the status bar in Figure 7.3, prompting you to fill in anything that is missing.

2. You will be asked how many or how much of the material you need. Enter a numeric value and press Enter.

3. SAP R/3 displays another "guiding" question, this time asking you to enter a delivery date. Enter a future delivery date in the format specified by your company. Then tab to Plnt.

4. Enter a valid Plant code and press Enter. SAP R/3 accepts the complete entry. As you can see in Figure 7.4, some of the fields for the first line item are now shaded. This tells you that the first line has been accepted.

 TIP **Date Format** In Lesson 19, "Customizing Your User ID," you will learn to specify the date format you want to use. The format that you pick will have no effect on how SAP R/3 stores the date internally. Customizing the format simply affects the way the date will be presented for your individual User Name. (Note, however, that your company may set a standard date format for you to use in SAP R/3.)

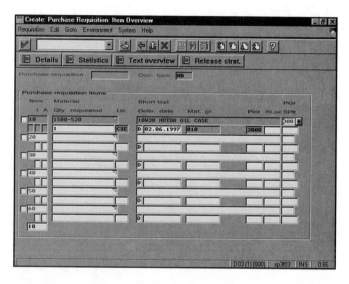

FIGURE 7.4   One line item has been accepted.

5. Add another line item to the requisition, asking for more of the same product to be delivered on a different date. Simply tab down to the second Material field and start entering the next line as you did the first.

6. Press Enter when you are done. The requisition now has two items.

DON'T FORGET THE DETAILS

Suppose you want to store some more detailed information related to the second line item. For example, you might want to mark the purchase requisition so that this particular material comes to your attention when it arrives. Follow these steps to add those details (or others) to the purchase requisition.

1. Click the item selection box beside Item #2 on the requisition. This tells SAP R/3 that the next instruction applies only to the second line item, and not the first.

2. Click the Details screen button, and the Create Purchase
   Requisition: Item details screen shown in Figure 7.5
   appears. You can see by the value in the Item field that
   this screen applies to the second line item.

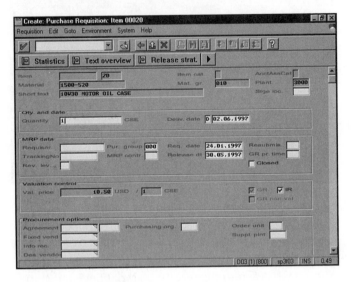

FIGURE 7.5   A details screen.

3. Tab down to the Requisnr field and enter your name (so
   that the material will come to your attention).

4. Click the Back button to return to the Create Purchase
   Requisition: Item Overview screen.

5. Click the Save button on the toolbar. SAP R/3 saves the
   details and returns you to the initial screen, where you
   can enter the next requisition.

When you save this document, SAP R/3 displays a message in the
status bar informing you that a purchase requisition was created.
It also creates a purchase requisition number. Write down the
number your system gives you, since you will use it again in Lessons 9 and 10.

USING DEFAULT DATA

If you have a lot of similar records to enter, you can use default data to simplify your task. For example, in the Create Purchase Requisition: Initial Screen, you can enter data that will be the same for every item in the fields in the Default data for items box. So if you needed to create a batch of documents that are all for Plant 3000 and Purchasing Group 014, you could enter those values into the default data fields as shown in Figure 7.6.

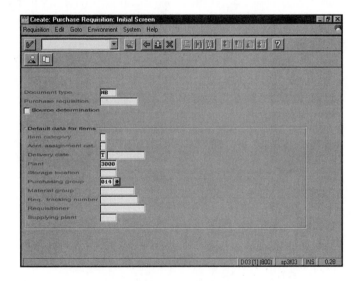

FIGURE 7.6   Using the default data fields.

When you finish filling in all of the default data, press Enter, and the Create Purchase Requisition: Item Overview screen reappears. For every line item on the purchase requisition, SAP R/3 has filled in the fields for which you supplied default data. All you have to do is fill in the other fields as you learned to do earlier in this lesson.

Take Advantage of SAP   Don't be afraid to press Enter
TIP   if you think that you are finished with a task—SAP R/3 will
guide you to fill in any missing information.

In this lesson, you learned how to create a business document for
which you already knew the values for the required fields. (The
example you used was the Purchase Requisition, but the principles are the same for other business documents. The key is to let
SAP R/3 guide you.) In the next lesson, you will learn how to use
matchcodes to look up values for fields.

USING MATCHCODES

In this lesson, you will learn how to use matchcodes to have SAP R/3 look up records for you.

USER REQUIREMENTS FOR THIS LESSON

For this lesson, you will need one of the following:

- A user logon name with authority to create a purchase requisition

- An application area where you have authority to create a document. You will create a Purchase Requisition as the example.

The way SAP R/3 uses matchcodes when you create this document is representative of how it uses them when you create (or display or change) other documents.

EXPLORING MATCHCODES

SAP R/3 uses matchcodes so you don't have to remember all the codes used for different items in your organization. You can have SAP R/3 look up items such as Product Numbers or Purchasing Groups.

 Matchcode   A tool you can use to have SAP R/3 locate the field values corresponding to selected items.

- Any field that displays a small triangle in the top-right corner has a matchcode (see Figure 8.1).

- When you move your cursor to one of these fields, the down-arrow appears beside it.

This Matchcode indicator appears when your cursor is in the field

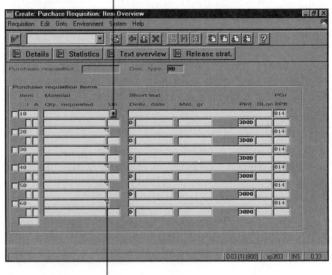

Matchcodes are available for these fields

Figure 8.1   Some fields have matchcodes available.

Are There Matchcodes?   Even if there is no triangle, that does not necessarily mean there are no matchcodes. The only way to be sure is to tab to the field and press F4 (Possible Entries). SAP R/3 either presents a matchcode list or tells you they are not available.

Work through the following exercise to learn firsthand how to use matchcodes.

1. Start from the Create Purchase Requisition: Item Overview Screen (which you worked with in the last lesson).

2. Move your cursor to the Material field for one of the line
   items.

3. Click the down arrow beside the field or press F4, and SAP
   R/3 displays a Selection of Search Method dialog box like
   the one shown in Figure 8.2. Which *Matchcode ID* you use
   depends on what you know about the material.

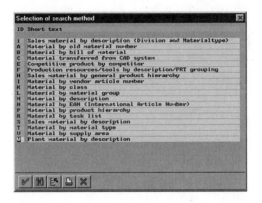

FIGURE 8.2   SAP R/3 asks which matchcode it should use.

Matchcode IDs   A system by which SAP R/3 distin-
guishes between several different matchcodes that may
be available for a field. In the example in Figure 8.2 ,
Matchcode ID 'K' would help you find a material number
for which you know the material class.

4. Let's assume you know the material description. Double-
   click matchcode W, Material by description, and a Restrict
   Value Range dialog box appears (see Figure 8.3).

TIP   **Consolidating Codes**   Some companies, when they install SAP R/3, take advantage of the opportunity to consolidate the way products are numbered. For example, if Marketing uses one set of numbers for a particular product and Manufacturing uses another set for the same product, SAP R/3 can accommodate both sets of users until everyone understands the new consolidated numbers. (Some of the earlier numbers may be carried on in a field called "Old Material number.")

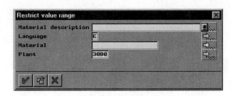

FIGURE 8.3   A Restrict Value Range dialog box will narrow down the search.

5. You can enter information into any of the fields presented to narrow down the search, and then click Enter. (For our example, just click Enter.) A window appears, listing the values you have to choose from (see Figure 8.4).

6. Double-click the material you want to include in your Purchase Requisition. SAP R/3 takes you back to the Create Purchase Requisition: Item Overview screen. Notice that the correct Material code has been inserted into the field.

7. Press Enter, and SAP R/3 fills in the other fields. Because this product is listed on the material master, SAP R/3 "recognizes it" and supplies the appropriate short text, Unit of measure, and Material Group.

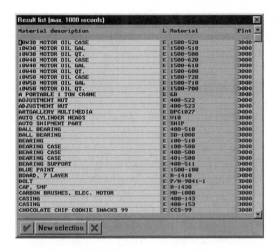

FIGURE 8.4 Choose a material number.

Go with the Flow   If you don't know whether or not
you've completed a screen, press Enter; SAP R/3 will
indicate the screen's status on the message line. (For
example, it might let you know that you need to supply a
Purchasing Group or Plant.)

TIP

8. Even though there is no arrow and no triangle showing
   for Purchasing Group, there is still a matchcode list available for it. Tab over to the field and press F4.

9. Double-click an item to select it. You will be returned
   again to the Create Purchase Requisition: Item Overview
   screen.

10. If you continue to press Enter, you will be prompted for
    the missing items Quantity, Delivery date, and Plant.
    Enter a Quantity and Delivery date as you did in Lesson 7,
    "Creating a Document." When you have completed the
    required fields for the line item, the cursor advances to
    the next line. (This is how you know you've filled in all
    the required fields.)

11. When you've entered all the information, click the Exit
toolbutton. If you've made changes that you haven't
saved yet, SAP R/3 displays the Exit document dialog box.
Click Yes if you want to save the document and then exit;
click No if you want to discard the document and exit.
(You can click Cancel if you decide you don't really want
to exit after all.)

Dialog Box Caution   Dialog boxes like this one can
TIP prevent you from accidentally losing your work. Never let
responding to them become a habit. Follow this simple
proverb: "Engage brain before clicking mouse."

TEXT SEARCHING AND WILDCARDS

SAP R/3 also allows you to search text fields by using *wildcards*.
For example, if you didn't know a product number for the material you need, but you did know it was something for a motor,
you could use a wildcard to find the material code (see Figure 8.5).

Wildcard   In poker, this is a card you can use to represent any card. In SAP R/3, a wildcard is a character
you can use to represent any character or series of
characters.

To learn how to use a wildcard, follow these steps to find the
matchcode for an unknown material:

1. From the Selection of Search Method list for the Material
field (shown in Figure 8.2) , double-click M, Material by
description. A Restrict Value Range dialog box appears.

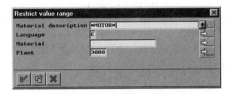

FIGURE 8.5   You use the wildcards in the Restrict Value Range box.

2. For the example described above, you want to look for all records that contain the word "MOTOR." Type ***MOTOR***. (In general, type any word that corresponds to your company's list, surrounded by the * wildcard characters.)

3. Click Continue. SAP R/3 displays only those materials whose descriptions contain "MOTOR" (see Figure 8.6). Notice that the Material code you used in the previous lesson (1500–520 for 10-W-30 motor oil) appears on the list.

FIGURE 8.6   A "filtered list."

4. Double-click the code to carry it back to the Create Purchase Requisition: Item Overview screen.

SAP R/3 remembers the last matchcode ID you used and auto-matically takes you back to the Restrict Value Range dialog box that you last used. If you need to get to the Selection of Search Methods box again, click the New Search icon shown in Figure 8.7

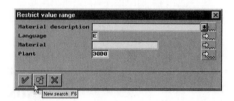

FIGURE 8.7   New Search takes you back to the Selection of Search Methods box.

OTHER WAYS

Although there may be many matchcodes for a single field, they all lead to the same table of values. There are just different ways of searching. Some other ways of opening a matchcode list include:

- When your cursor is in the field for which you want a matchcode, Press F4.

- Click the down arrow icon beside the field.

- Right-click anywhere on the screen, and then select F4 Matchcodes from the list displayed.

In this lesson, you learned how to access and use matchcodes to help you find values for fields. In the next lesson, you will learn how to display a document.

DISPLAYING A DOCUMENT

In this lesson, you will learn how to look up and display a document directly with the document number and also by using matchcodes.

USER REQUIREMENTS FOR THIS LESSON

For this lesson, you will need one of the following:

- The number of the document you created in Lesson 8.

- A user name with authority to display Purchase Requisitions.

- A user name with authority to display another business document so that you can follow along.

Display Access Only? Sometimes a user name is authorized to view a type of business document but is not authorized to create or change that type of document.

DIRECT LOOK-UP

Most kinds of business document have a reference number, such as a Purchase Requisition number or an Invoice number. When you know the number, you can use it directly to display the document.

1. From the Purchasing screen, choose Requisition, Display. The Display Purchase Requisition: Initial screen appears.

2. Enter the Purchase Requisition number you recorded from Lesson 7 in the Purchase requisition field (see Figure 9.1).

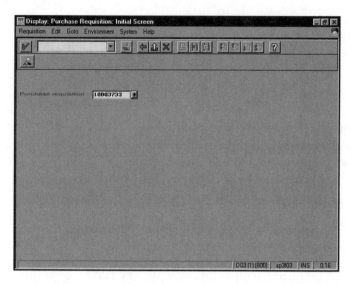

FIGURE 9.1   When you know the number, you can enter it here.

3. Press Enter, and the Display Purchase Requisition: Item
   Overview screen appears. As you can see in Figure 9.2, the
   fields are shaded (not white). This is SAP R/3's way of
   telling you that these fields are display-only; you cannot
   type in them. The only fields not shaded are the item
   selection boxes and the starting line-item field (the white
   boxes to the left and in the white box in the lower-left
   corner).

TIP   **The Starting Line-Item Field**   The screen normally lists
approximately the first eight line items on the document,
starting with line-item 1. However, if you type **50** into this
field and press Enter, your display will start with line-item
50 instead. This makes it easier to work with long documents in which many line items are listed, or to go to an
item in a long requisition.

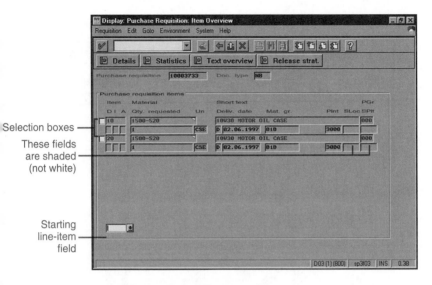

Selection boxes ——

These fields
are shaded
(not white) ——

Starting
line-item ——
field

FIGURE 9.2   Displaying the line items.

4. Click the selection box beside the second item to display
   more detail, and then click the Details screen-button. The
   Display Purchase Requisition: Item 00020 screen appears
   (see Figure 9.3).

   Figure 9.3 shows the same item you saw on line 2 of the
   previous screen, but with more fields showing. (Notice
   that the line item number (20) shows in the title bar.) In
   this format, all of the fields are display-only.

TIP   **Viewing Multiple Line Items**   If you want to see several
of the line items, you can click all of their selection boxes,
and then browse through them in sequence by clicking
the Details screen-button and pressing Enter after each
item.

The line item number

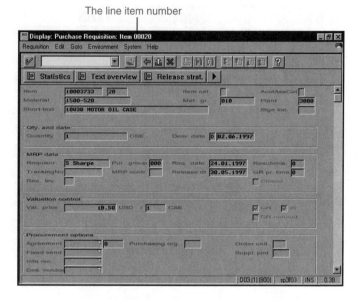

FIGURE 9.3   We are looking at the details for line item 20.

5. Click the Exit button on the toolbar to return to the Purchasing screen.

Accessing Different Screens   Different kinds of screens may be associated with every kind of document and are accessible from screen-buttons. One of the additional screens available in the current example is the Text Overview screen. (For more details on text entry, see Lesson 14.)

Additional Screens   Just because SAP R/3 provides the additional screens does not mean you need to use them at your company or for every kind of record.

LOOK-UP WITH MATCHCODES

Sometimes, you may not know the number of the document you
want to display. You can also locate a document using matchcodes. Follow these step to open and display the same document
using matchcodes.

1. From the Purchasing screen (where you were at the end of
   the previous task), choose Requisition, Display to access
   the Display Purchase Requisition: Initial screen (same as
   Figure 9.1).

2. Click the down arrow next to the field, and either a
   Matchcode ID dialog box or a Restrict Value Ranges dialog box appears (see Figure 9.4).

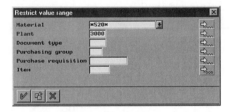

FIGURE 9.4   Enter the search values.

 Wrong Dialog Box?   If the wrong Restrict Value Ranges
dialog box appears, click the New Search button to go to
the Selection of Search Methods box.

 No Records?   Inevitably, when you work with SAP R/3,
you will sometimes select a matchcode for which there
are no records. When that happens, SAP R/3 displays an
error message on the status line, informing you that **No
Matchcode record was found**. This is normal; just pick a
different matchcode.

3. Enter more specific search criteria (in our example, we entered *520* for Material) and click Continue. SAP R/3 displays a list of the Purchase Requisitions that match the criteria you typed in the Restrict Value Ranges box (see Figure 9.6).

 Restricting Values Is Optional You don't *have* to type anything in this box, it just produces a shorter list for you.

4. Double-click the line containing the record you want to display, or click the line and then click the Enter button. You should see the Display Purchase Requisition: Initial screen with the value you selected from the matchcode list carried into the field.

5. To display the document, follow the steps for using the Direct Look-Up method (earlier in the lesson).

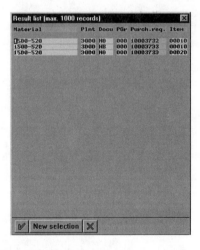

FIGURE 9.6 Choose from this list.

In this lesson, you learned how to display a document by typing its number and by locating it with a matchcode list. You also learned that you can move between several screens associated with a document by using the screen-buttons. In the next lesson, you will learn how to find and change a document.

CHANGING A DOCUMENT

In this lesson, you will learn how to find and change a document that's already on your system.

USER REQUIREMENTS FOR THIS LESSON

For this lesson, you will need one of the following:

- The number of the document you created in Lesson 7

- A user name with authority to change Purchase Requisitions

- A user name with authority to change another business document

FINDING THE DOCUMENT

Regardless of the kind of document you want to change, the process is similar. You bring the document up on your screen, make the changes, and save it.

For the example in this lesson, you're going to work with a Purchase Requisition. Therefore, you'll begin from the main Purchasing screen again.

1. Choose Requisition, Change, and the Change: Purchase Requisition: Initial Screen appears.

2. Type the document number for the document you want to open, or choose it from the matchcode list as you did in Lesson 9.

3. Press Enter. The Change: Purchase Requisition: Item Overview screen appears. Figure 10.1 shows that screen.

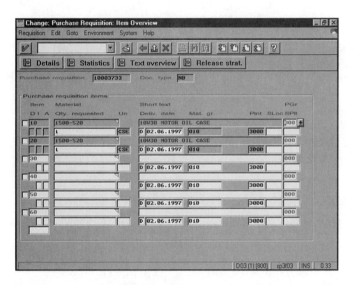

FIGURE 10.1   You can edit the document from this screen if the field you need to change is displayed here.

 Similar Screens   Note that the Change: Purchase Requisition screen is almost identical to the Display Purchase Requisition screen.

CHANGING A LINE ITEM

Suppose for a minute that you have just been promoted. (Doesn't that feel good!) As a result of your promotion, your job responsibilities have changed. Now the material you ordered in Lesson 7 should go to the attention of the unfortunate person who is taking over your old job. You need to edit the Purchase Requisition to reflect this change. Follow these steps to work through changing a document:

1. Click the selection box beside line item 2 to work with that item. A dot appears in the box, confirming your selection.

2. Click the Details screen button, and the Change: Purchase Requisition: Item 00020 screen (shown in Figure 10.2) appears.

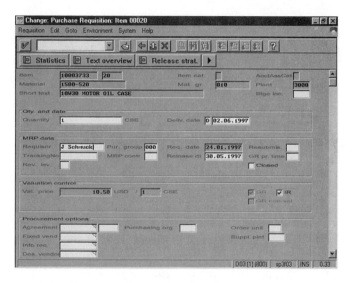

FIGURE 10.2   You can change the details from here.

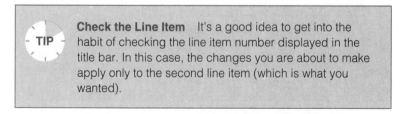

Check the Line Item   It's a good idea to get into the habit of checking the line item number displayed in the title bar. In this case, the changes you are about to make apply only to the second line item (which is what you wanted).

3. Click in the Requisnr. field and enter the name of the person who is to be notified when the material arrives.

4. Click the Save button on the toolbar to save your changes. SAP R/3 displays a confirmation message like this one in the status bar:

Purchase requisition 10000014 has been changed

Quick Change   If you need to change one of the item fields that appear on the Change: Purchase Requisition: Item Overview screen (shown in Figure 10.1), you can change it directly on that screen and click the Save toolbutton. You only need to go to the Item Detail screen (shown in Figure 10.2) if the field you need to change is not on the Change: Purchase Requisition: Item Overview screen.

ADDING AND DELETING LINE ITEMS

Sometimes you need to add or delete individual line items on a document.

To add a line item, follow these steps:

1. Go to the Change: Purchase Requisition: Item Overview screen as you learned earlier in this lesson.

2. Place your cursor in the first field of the first empty line item and begin filling in data. (In the case of the sample Purchase Requisition, it is the **Material** field for line item **3**.)

Those Item Numbers   You can skip over the Item field and just let SAP R/3 take care of the line item numbers. SAP R/3 proposes that the third line item should be (are you ready for this?) number 3. Unless you have a compelling reason to make it something else, there is no need to change it.

3. Click the Save toolbutton to save your requisition with the new line item added.

To delete a line item, follow these steps:

1. In the Change: Purchase Requisition: Item Overview
   screen (shown in Figure 10.2), click the selection box
   beside the line item you want to delete.

2. Pull down the Edit menu and choose Delete.

3. Click the Save toolbutton to save your Purchase Requisition with the line deleted.

In this lesson, you learned how to change records that already
exist on your system. In the next lesson, you will learn how to use
List displays.

11 USING LIST DISPLAY

In this lesson, you will learn how to select and display lists of documents.

USER REQUIREMENTS FOR THIS LESSON

For this lesson, you need to know the document number you created in Lesson 7 so that you can choose selection criteria that include that particular item.

For the examples in this lesson, you will use a purchase requisition as your sample document to display lists. It is typical of other documents you can look up on SAP R/3.

REPORTING WITH LIST DISPLAY

This lesson shows you how to display a list of documents. Because you normally need to see only part of a list, it shows you how to limit the list. Some people use this to limit their list, say, to requisitions for their division only.

1. From the Purchasing screen, choose Requisitions, List Display, General. The List Display of Purchase Requisitions screen appears (see Figure 11.1).

Ranges You will usually want to specify a range of values on this screen. Use the left column for the starting value and the right column for the ending value. Just use the Purchase requisition number From and To fields for now.

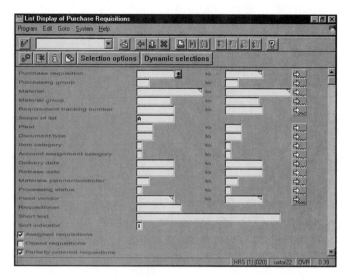

FIGURE 11.1   You can narrow down your request with this
screen.

 2. Type a range of requisition numbers here that you know
        contains the number of the requisition you created in
        Lesson 7. Then click the Execute button. SAP displays the
        list of purchase requisitions. Figure 11.2 shows a typical
        list.

 Matchcodes   Note that some of the fields have
matchcodes that you could use to look up values to insert. Some of the fields, even though they don't display
the triangle, do have possible entries available. Purchasing group is one of these. You can choose to enter values
in any combination of fields to limit the list display. Or you
can choose to display all records by not filling in any
fields.

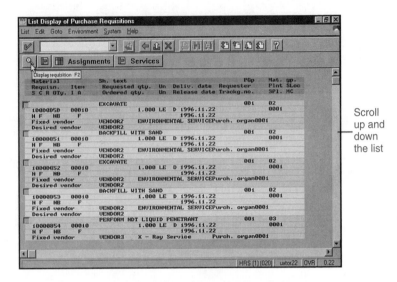

Scroll
up and
down
the list

FIGURE 11.2   The top of the list you asked for.

Stacked Fields Note that there are several screen lines for each record in this list. SAP R/3 makes it easier for you to see which fields belong to which record by shading the lines in groups. In addition, some of the field titles are abbreviated, and they are stacked, as they were in Lesson 3. Again, if you are unsure of what one of the abbreviated names means, click it and then click Field Level Help.

3. To get a better look at a requisition, click on it and click the Display Requisition toolbutton. SAP R/3 displays a detail screen similar to the one in Figure 11.3 for the requisition you selected.

4. Click the Back toolbutton to get back to the List Display of Purchase Requisitions screen.

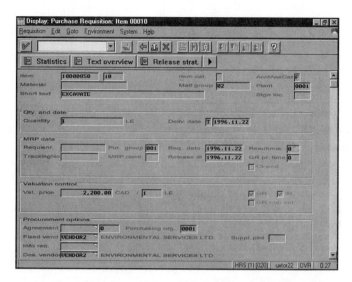

FIGURE 11.3   You can also get to any of the other information screens related to this requisition by clicking the appropriate toolbutton or selecting from the Goto menu.

5. From the List Display of Purchase Requisitions screen, click a line and click the Detail icon. SAP shows you the details of the selected requisition, in a screen like the one shown in Figure 11.4.

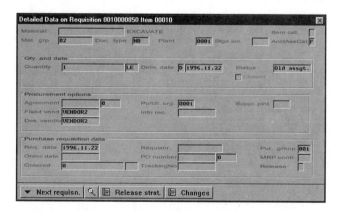

FIGURE 11.4   Note that you could click Next Requisition to scroll through the items one at a time.

6. To close the dialog box, click the Close (X) button. Then click the Back toolbutton to return to the List Display of Purchase Requisitions screen.

MORE POWERFUL SELECTIONS

Extended selections screens allow you to limit the list display in almost any way you can imagine. Assume, for example, that you are responsible for all Plants between 400 and 500, except for 404 (which is somebody else's responsibility). You could fill in 400–500 as a range, and enter 404 as a single value exclusion.

Let's take another look at the List Display of Purchase Requisitions screen. You can use it to do some very powerful selections.

1. Position your cursor on the Multiple Selection icon, and a Quick info box appears. Click Multiple Selection. The Multiple Selection screen appears (see Figure 11.5).

2. You can type whatever values you need into this screen. For example, ask the system to include entries for Plant 337 and for any other Plant in the range of 100 to 200 (except in the range 150–160). To do so, fill in value ranges for Plant as 100–200 and 150–160. Leaving your cursor in the "160" box, click the Options button. The Plant: Maintain Selection Options dialog box appears (see Figure 11.6). This box applies to whatever range your cursor was in when you clicked Options.

3. Select the Outside Range option to exclude the range between the specified values. With the values shown, for example, you are telling SAP R/3 to "Exclude values in the range of 150 to 160."

4. Click the check mark button, and you are returned to the Multiple Selection for Plant dialog box. The range you entered for exclusion appears in the Ranges section at the bottom of the dialog box, as shown in Figure 11.7.

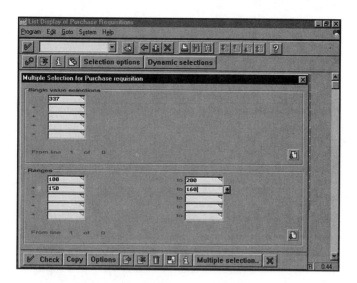

FIGURE 11.5   The Multiple Selection screen.

FIGURE 11.6   You can choose ranges to be included or excluded.

This extended selection exists throughout SAP R/3. If you are responsible for products with certain numbers, employees at a certain location, or retail outlets in a certain area, this may be the tool you need to narrow down your list displays.

Saving It   You can save long or complex selections for use again later. You can also share them with other SAP R/3 users, and you can use extended selections saved by others. See Lesson 13, "Using Variants," for more information.

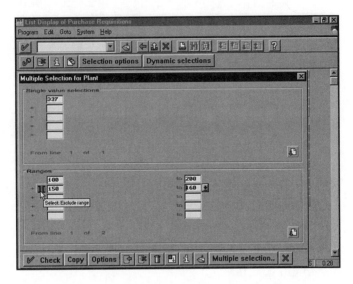

FIGURE 11.7   An exclusion range.

In this lesson, you learned how to display lists of records. You also learned how to enter selection criteria to limit these lists. In the next lesson, you will learn how to generate and print reports.

GENERATING REPORTS AND PRINTING

In this lesson, you learn how to print lists and reports in SAP R/3. You will also learn how SAP R/3 defines output destinations for business documents such as Purchase Orders, Invoices, Production Orders, and so on.

WHAT YOU NEED FOR THIS LESSON

For this lesson, you need a material number for which several Purchase Orders have been created on your system.

SELECTING AND GENERATING REPORTS

For this example, you will use a Purchase Order, or an item that has been approved for purchase.

> **TIP** **Routing** Output is routed in two different ways: by your User ID (for lists and reports) and by predefined destination (for business documents).

1. From the Purchasing screen, select Purchase Order, Reporting, General Analyses. A screen similar to the one in Figure 12.1 appears.

2. You must supply at least one value in the Main Selection Criteria area. For now, use a material number that you know is on existing Purchase Requisitions. (Be sure the Date range you use is wide enough to find your document.) Then press Enter. As you can see in Figure 12.2, SAP displays the name of your material at the top of your

screen. The body of the report contains one line for every purchase order line item for the material you selected.

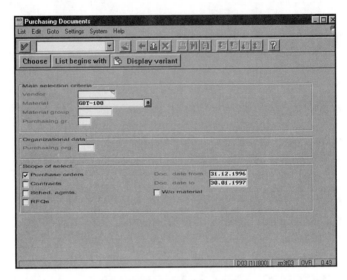

FIGURE 12.1 You can use this screen to limit your report in a variety of ways.

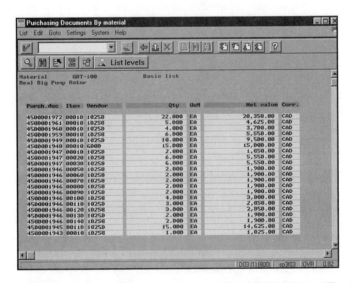

FIGURE 12.2 In this demo system, material GBT-100 is a "Real Big Pump Rotor."

Data Behind Data   This list is a wolf in sheep's clothing.
TIP   There is an amazing amount of detail behind it. Try
double-clicking a Purch.doc number (PO number); SAP
R/3 displays the original PO. Then click the Back
toolbutton to get back to the report.

 3. Click the Sort icon to see how SAP R/3 will sort your report. The Sort dialog box appears (see Figure 12.3.) The
Sort dialog box enables you to do subsorts. For example,
you could choose Vendor as the first sort and Plant as the
second. This would produce a list sorted first by Vendor
and then, within Vendor, sorted by Plant.

FIGURE 12.3   Experiment with some different sort combinations.

4. Set your sort options and then click the check mark button. SAP rearranges the items in the list based on the sort
order you selected.

 5. When you are finished with sorts (but while the report
lines are still displayed on your screen), click the Total
button. The Total Variants dialog box appears (see
Figure 12.4).

Figure 12.4 The box shows the active variant and lists the other variants for which you can total the items in the list.

6. Double-click Purchasing Document Totals, and a summarized list like the one in Figure 12.5 appears.

Drilling for Data If you see a line with several items on it (look in the Number column), you can double-click that PO number to drill down to the detail behind it. When you finish, click the Back toolbutton to return to your report.

7. Click the List + subtots toolbutton, and SAP displays the list with subtotals, as shown in Figure 12.6.

8. Finally, click the List Levels toolbar button to see an overview of generated list levels similar to the one in Figure 12.7. The third item on the list (item 2) is highlighted, indicating that it is the one you were on when you clicked List Levels.

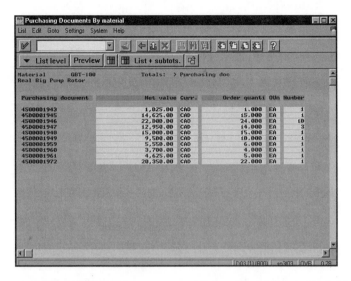

FIGURE 12.5   SAP R/3 has summed the value of this material for each purchase order that contains it.

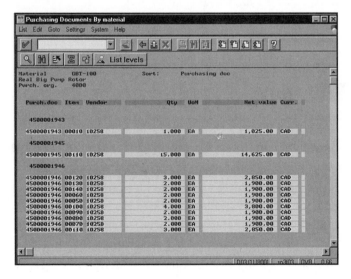

FIGURE 12.6   A list with subtotals.

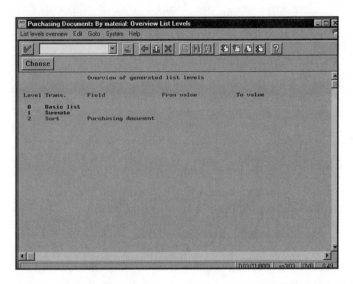

FIGURE 12.7 The levels of list that you have generated. The third item on the list (item 2) is highlighted, indicating that it is the one you were on when you clicked List Levels.

9. Click any of the other items to recall an earlier list.

PRINTING

With all the powerful capabilities that generating reports allows you, the need to print is almost made redundant. Still, there will be times when you need a hard copy of your reports. Follow these steps to print reports:

1. Using the previous steps, set up the report you want. When the report is displayed on your screen, choose List, Print. The Print Screen List screen appears (see Figure 12.8).

2. If you know the name of your local printer, enter it here. If not, choose it from the matchcode list.

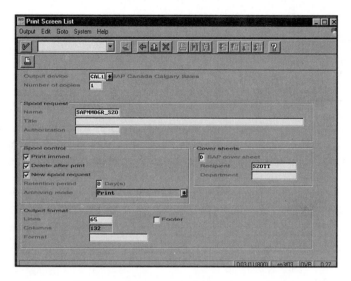

FIGURE 12.8 Select a printer and set printing options.

 Where Did These Settings Come From? If you have assigned defaults to your User ID, those values will be carried through into some of the fields. If you don't want to use the defaults, you can go in and change the default values proposed on the Print Screen List.

3. If you select the Print Immed. option, SAP prints the report on the selected printer. If you don't select Print Immed., SAP generates a *spool request*. This request will be held by the *output controller* for printing later.

4. When you are ready to print, click the Print icon. You will get a message something like **Spool request (number *XXXXX*) created**.

Spool Request   This is a saved print job.

Output Controller   A program that runs on the central computer to control all the spool requests.

You can access the output controller from any screen by choosing System, Services, Output Controller. From the resulting screen, you can print, change, delete, display, or check the status of spool requests.

TIP

Learning More   To learn more about using the output controller, choose Help, Getting Started from Any Screen. From the Getting Started with R/3 help screen, scroll down to Printing and click it. In the box that appears, click Managing Spool Requests from the Output Controller.

In this lesson, you learned how SAP R/3 handles printing and output. You also learned that you can change its proposed settings for your User ID at the time of printing. In the next lesson, you will learn how to use variants to save time when you have large or complex selection criteria for your lists and reports. You will also learn how you can save and share these selection criteria with other users.

USING VARIANTS

13

In this lesson, you learn how to use variants to save time when you have large or complex selection criteria for your lists and reports. You also learn how you can save and share your selection criteria with other users.

WHAT YOU NEED FOR THIS LESSON

For this lesson, you need access to a report or list that has extended selection criteria available. (You learned how to specify extended selection criteria in Lesson 11, "Using List Display.")

CREATING AND SAVING VARIANTS

A *variant* is a saved set of selection criteria. You can use these criteria for lists and reports. You can create variants for your own use, and you can share them with others.

Two Meanings! The word variant has one other meaning in SAP R/3. Within Production Planning, it is used to describe products that are built with different options. For example, a Ford with an automatic transmission is a variant of a Ford with a manual transmission. That kind of variant is a separate topic and will not be covered here. If you need to know more about PP variants, choose Help, Help Library, Production Planning, Variants.

Suppose your area of responsibility includes Purchasing groups 11, 14, 19, and 53 through 72. You might want to see requisitions for these areas only. Follow these steps to learn how:

1. From the Purchasing screen, choose Requisitions, List Display, General. The List Display of Purchase Requisitions screen appears.

2. Click the extended selection criteria arrow (beside the Purchasing Group). The Multiple Selection for Purchasing Group screen appears (see Figure 13.1).

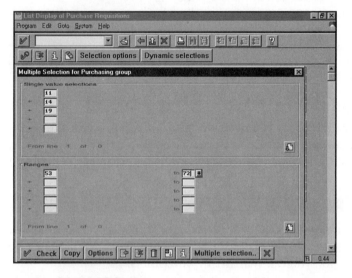

FIGURE 13.1 These Multiple selections can get long and complex; notice the Page down symbols in both areas of the screen.

3. Fill in the boxes with the values shown in Figure 13.1 to see requisitions for your purchasing groups only. (You can use the selection criteria in a similar way for any other field.)

4. When you finish, click the Copy button to return to the List Display of Purchase Requisitions screen.

5. Next, open the Goto menu, choose Variants, and then choose Save As Variant (see Figure 13.2). The ABAP/4: Save as Variant screen appears. SAP R/3 prompts you for the name and description you would like to use to save your selection criteria.

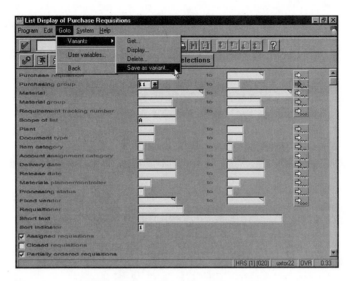

FIGURE 13.2   Saving a variant.

6. Enter the required information, as shown in Figure 13.3, and press Enter. SAP R/3 displays a message that the variant you created has been saved.

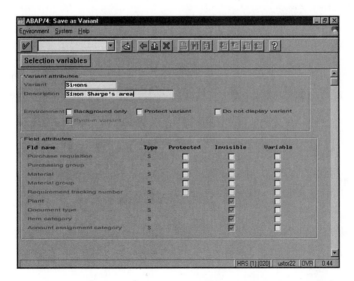

FIGURE 13.3   Choose a name and description for the variant.

7. Exit the List Display of Purchase Requisitions screen by
clicking the X (Cancel) toolbutton. From the Purchasing
screen, re-open the list by choosing Requisition, List Display, General.

8. Click the Get Variant button, and SAP R/3 displays a list
of all variants for List Display of Purchase Requisitions
that you have access to (see Figure 13.4). In this case,
there is only one variant on the list, the one we just
saved. In your case, however, there could already be more
variants.

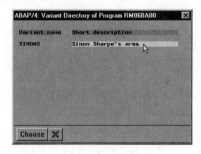

Figure 13.4   Choose a variant from the list (in this case, there's
only one).

9. Double-click the variant you want to reload, and you are
returned to the List Display of Purchase Requisitions
screen. As you can see in Figure 13.5, the screen now contains all of the criteria you keyed in and saved earlier. The
colored arrow beside the second Purchasing group tells
you that extended selection criteria are in effect for that
field.

You create and save variants the same way, regardless of what
fields and which selection criteria you use.

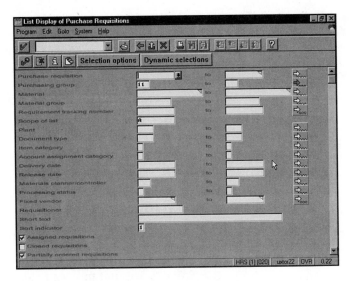

FIGURE 13.5   An extended selection is in effect.

In this lesson, you learned how to use variants to save time when you have large or complex selection criteria for your lists and reports. You also learned how you can save and share these selection criteria with other users. In the next lesson, you will learn how to include long text descriptions with a record and how to edit that text.

14 EDITING TEXT

In this lesson, you learn to edit text using SAP R/3's built-in text editor.

WHAT YOU NEED FOR THIS LESSON

- The number of a requisition you can edit

ADDING AND EDITING TEXT

You can add text to most documents to highlight any special processing or conditions that SAP R/3 does not provide fields for. Some people use this in the same way they use sticky notes to draw attention to some unusual condition they need to remain aware of. To add text to a document, follow these steps:

1. Start at the Purchasing screen and choose Requisition, Change. Type the requisition number and press Enter. The Change: Purchase Requisition: Item Overview screen (shown in Figure 14.1) appears.

2. Click the line you want to select, and then click the Text Overview button to get into the text screen (see Figure 14.2). If you want to attach a short message to the requisition, you enter it in this screen. (Note that different kinds of records provide different numbers of types and text fields.)

3. Type your note into one of the fields provided and click the Save toolbutton.

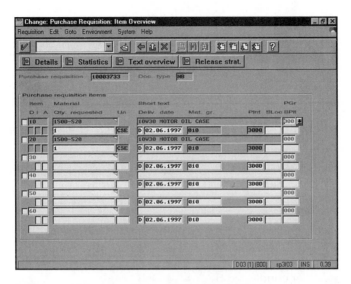

FIGURE 14.1 You can edit requisitions from here.

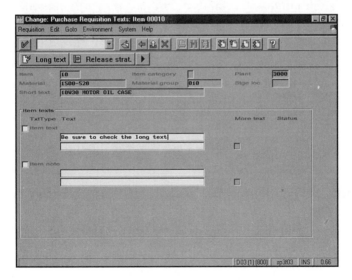

FIGURE 14.2 You can add short text here.

4. If you need to enter a longer passage of text associated with the record, click the Long Text button. SAP opens a text editor, and any short text you already entered for this record appears on the first line (see Figure 14.3).

Keep Your Word Processor! This text editor is not likely to replace your favorite word processor, but it is useful for entering text. You could spend a lot of time learning all the things it can do, but the three basics are adding text, deleting text, and inserting text.

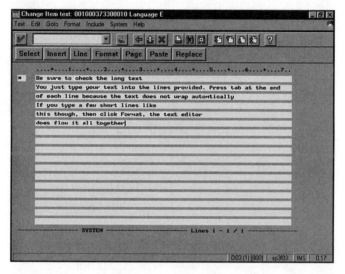

FIGURE 14.3   The short text you just entered is carried through to the first line.

5. Add and edit text in the text editor using the following techniques:

   • **To add text...**   Enter some text (as shown in Figure 14.3). You can't type past the end of the line, so press Tab when you get close to the end. Type all of your text, pressing Tab as necessary to move from

field to field. When you finish entering text, click
the Format toolbutton to flow the text lines together.

- **To delete text...**   Highlight the text you want to
  delete and click Delete. If necessary, click the Format
  button to flow the text back together.

- **To insert text...**   Move your cursor to the insertion point and click Insert. SAP breaks the text to
  make room for the new text. Your screen will look
  similar to the one in Figure 14.4. Enter your text and
  click End Insertion to flow the text together.

- **To start a new paragraph...**   Press Enter if you
  want to put text on a new line. SAP moves down to
  the next line, and an asterisk appears to the left of
  the line to show that it's a separate paragraph. Lines
  after the asterisk will not be flowed in with the previous lines when you press Format. However, you
  can delete the asterisk and click Format if you decide
  you want to join the lines.

It Doesn't Flow   You must move to the next line with
your Tab key (not the Enter key) if you want to be able to
flow the lines together when you finish.

6. When you finish entering and editing the long text, click
   the Back toolbutton to return to the short text screen. A
   check mark in the More Text box indicates there is a long
   text message associated with this Purchase Requisition
   (see Figure 14.5).

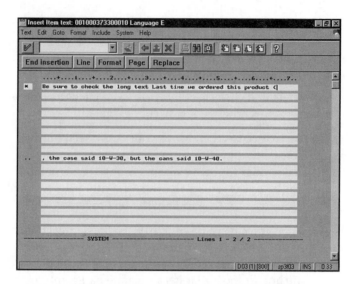

FIGURE 14.4 SAP provides empty lines for your new text.

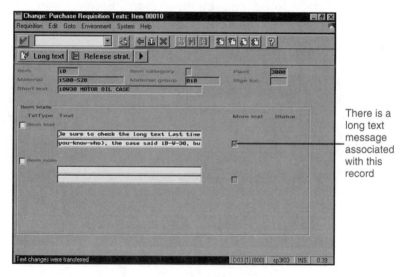

There is a long text message associated with this record

FIGURE 14.5 This is the only place SAP tells you of the message.

7. SAP displays a message at the bottom of the screen saying **Text changes were transferred**. Click the Save toolbutton to save your changes, and you'll see a message saying **Purchase requisition *xxxx* changed**.

In this lesson, you learned how to add to and change both short text and long text messages in a business document. In the next lesson, you will learn what master data is and how to view it or change it.

15 USING MASTER DATA

In this lesson, you will learn what master data is and how to use and maintain it. You will also learn what kinds of master data are available in SAP R/3.

WHAT YOU NEED FOR THIS LESSON

For this lesson, you will need one of the following:

- A user logon name with authority to change a Material Master record
- A material number

For this example, you will use a Material record as your sample master file. It is typical of other master files you create on SAP R/3. Changing other master files is similar.

KINDS OF DATA

In very general terms, there are two kinds of data in any system:

- **Transaction Data** This represents the normal day-to-day business transactions in a system. If you couldn't create these documents, your business would come to a stop. Purchase Orders, Invoices, and Production Orders are all examples of movement data. These are discussed in more detail in Lesson 22, "Kinds of Business Documents."

- **Master data** This data is relatively fixed in your system. Your company might be able to run for days without creating new master data. Customer Master, Personnel Master, and Chart of Accounts are all examples of master data. Note, however, that not all master data has the word "Master" in its name.

The authority to change master data is usually controlled more tightly than the authority to create transaction data. Most SAP R/3 users will not need to maintain master data. All users will have to use master data in one way or another.

MAINTAINING DATA IN A MASTER FILE

Maintaining data in a master file includes adding new records, deleting old records, and changing existing records. Here is how you change a record on the Material Master:

1. From the Main menu, choose Logistics, Materials Management, Material Master.

2. From Material Master, choose Material, Change, Immediately. With R/3, it is possible to set up a change ahead of time that will take effect on a certain date. The Change Material: Initial Screen appears (see Figure 15.1), asking you what material you want to change.

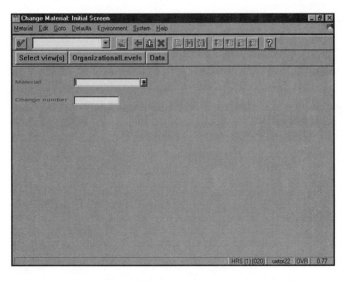

FIGURE 15.1   What material are you going to change?

3. You have probably guessed by now that you can key in
   the value directly or choose it from a matchcode list. Key
   in the value of a known material and press Enter. The
   Select View(s) dialog box shown in Figure 15.2 appears.

FIGURE 15.2   SAP R/3 has many views available.

 Your List Is Different?   Your installation may have created its own custom views for the material master, so you
may not get the same list that's shown here.

4. You can pick one or more of these views to control which
   fields are displayed to you. This is especially useful if only
   one particular field is important for your job (such as
   "weight" to a shipping clerk or "price" to a marketing
   rep). For now, pick Basic Data and click the check mark
   button. The Change Material: Basic Data screen appears
   (see Figure 15.3).

5. Scroll down to the Net Weight field (see Figure 15.4).
   Type **2** and press Enter. SAP displays this message in the
   message area: **The net weight is greater than the
   gross weight**. (It makes sense—the net is 2, and the
   gross is nothing.)

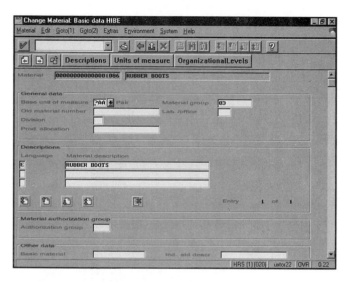

FIGURE 15.3   A material master record.

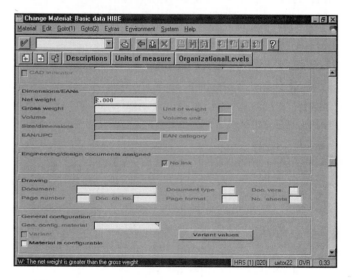

FIGURE 15.4   You can scroll down to see more fields.

6. In the Gross Weight field, type **3** and press Enter. SAP displays the message **Please specify relevant unit of weight**.

7. Enter a unit of weight (such as **KG**). Or, move to the Unit of Weight field, click the down arrow to access the list of valid entries on your system, and choose one of the entries.

8. Press Enter to clear the SAP R/3 data checks for this screen. SAP R/3 displays the dialog box shown in Figure 15.5.

Figure 15.5   Do you want to save your changes?

9. Click Yes to save your changes, and you get the message **Material XXXXXXXXX changed**.

List of Master Files

Table 15.1 lists some common master files used by various modules in SAP R/3. Most SAP R/3 users will see only a small number of these tables in their jobs. (For a description of the various SAP R/3 modules, refer to the appendices.)

Table 15.1   Common SAP Master Files

Name	Contents	R/3 Module
Asset Master	Managed assets	AM
Carrier Master	List of shipping companies	SD, MM
Chart of Accounts	Internal accounts to which debits and credits are charged	CO

NAME	CONTENTS	R/3 MODULE
Chart of Depreciation	Assets for which depreciation is accounted	AM
Customer Master	Customer name, address, credit terms, and so on	FI, SD, QM
Customer/Material info record	Describes material in customer's terms	SD
Equipment Master	Serial number, warranty info, and so on	PM
Functional Location Master	Locations where equipment can be installed	PM
Info-record	Vendor, Product	MM
Inspection Catalogs	General hierarchical list (attributes, possible defects, possible causes, and so on	QM
Inspection Methods	A predefined inspection operation	QM
Inspection Plan	A defined series of inspection operations	QM
Inventory Master	Material name, number in stock, storage location, and so on	MM, QM, PP, SD
Master Inspection Characteristics	Characteristics (color, weight, and so on) that define a material's quality	QM

continues

TABLE 15.1   CONTINUED

NAME	CONTENTS	R/3 MODULE
Material Master	Material number, characteristics, and so on	QM, SD, MM, PP
Outline Agreement	A contract to supply a variable amount of goods or services	SD
Personnel Master	Name, job, salary, and so on	HR
Routings	Sequences for production	PP
Test Equipment	Equipment used for quality management	QM
User Master	Users of SAP R/3 and what they are authorized to do	All
Vendor Master	Vendor name, address, contact, and so on	QM
Work Centers	Units where production processing takes place	QM, PP

In this lesson, you learned what master data is and how to maintain it. You saw that every module uses some kind of master data and that many master files are shared between modules. In the next lesson, you will learn how to use user parameters to cut down on the typing you have to do when creating new business documents.

Using User Parameters

In this lesson, you will learn how to use user parameters to cut down on the typing you need to do when creating new business documents.

What You Need for This Lesson

For this lesson, you need one of the following:

- A User ID with authority to create a purchase requisition

- A User ID with authority to create another business document so that you can follow along with the example

User Parameter A user parameter is something you set up to hold the value of a commonly used field. This will not effect other users; it applies only to your User ID. It also stays in effect for the next time you log on.

Setting Up the User Parameter

In SAP R/3, every field has a short code that the system uses to distinguish it from other fields. This code is called the PID (Parameter ID number). To set up a user parameter for a field, you need to know its PID number.

Finding the PID

The following steps walk you through finding the PID for a field (Purchasing Group, in this case) so you can set up the field's user parameter.

1. To begin, go to the Create: Purchase Requisition screen. Move your cursor down to the Purchasing Group field and click the Field Level Help toolbutton. A Help dialog box similar to the one in Figure 16.1 appears.

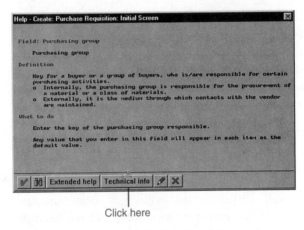

Click here

FIGURE 16.1   The first step to finding the PID number.

2. Click the Technical Info button, and the Technical Information dialog box appears. As you can see in Figure 16.2, this box contains the Parameter ID field. In this example, it contains the value "EKG."

TIP   **Copy—Don't Type!**   You could write down all the information in the Technical Information dialog box (or any other dialog box, for that matter), but the cut and paste approach is more efficient.

3. Move your cursor into the Parameter ID field and highlight the text (press and hold the mouse button and drag over the text). Figure 16.2 shows the field entry highlighted.

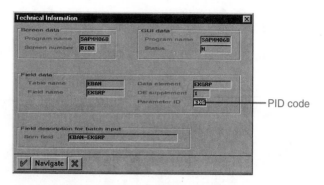

FIGURE 16.2   Finding the PID for a field.

4. Press and hold the Ctrl key and press C. (Ctrl+C is the shortcut key for the Copy command.) SAP copies the highlighted text to the *Clipboard*.

Clipboard   A temporary storage area for data you want to cut from one location and paste to another. You can also use it to cut and paste between other applications and SAP R/3.

5. Click the X (Cancel) button at the bottom of the dialog box to close it. Then do the same for the dialog box behind it.

SETTING THE PARAMETER

Now that you know the PID for the field, you can set its default value. To better understand how this can make your work easier, consider this scenario: If 99% of your work is in Purchasing organization #8, you could set that as the default through the Parameter ID. As a result, this field is filled in for you automatically, and 99% of the time, you don't have to enter anything for it. (Of course, you can always type over the default when necessary.) To set a default value:

1. To get to the screen where you set the default value for the user parameters from any screen, choose System, User Profile, User Parameters. The Maintain User: Parameters screen appears (see Figure 16.3).

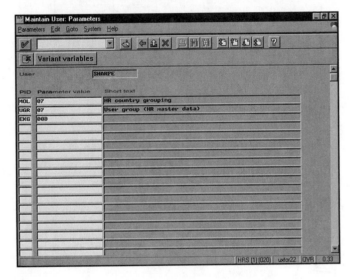

FIGURE 16.3   Add new user parameters here.

2. To tell SAP R/3 which field you are talking about, type the Parameter ID into the PID field. Or, if you copied it to the Clipboard in the previous steps, place the cursor in the PID field and press Ctrl+V. SAP pastes whatever is in the Clipboard (in this case, the PID for a purchasing group) in the PID field.

3. Next, move to the Parameter Value field and enter the value you want to carry through into your screens. (You don't need to enter anything in the Short Text field; it's just SAP's description of the field for which you are setting up a parameter.)

Changing Values   Don't worry about not being able to change the value later. When SAP R/3 uses a Parameter ID to fill in a field, it is just giving you a starting value. You can type over that value if you want to.

4. Click the Save toolbutton, and the status line tells you that your parameters were saved. Then click the Back toolbutton to return to the previous screen.

Maintaining Your User Parameters   You can set up as many fields as you want with default Parameter values. You can also delete any of them by highlighting the line, clicking Delete Line, and then clicking the Save toolbutton.

5. Now go to the Create Purchase Requisition screen. As you can see in Figure 16.4, the Purchasing Group field has been automatically filled in with the value 8, as you specified. (This value will be filled in on every screen that contains this field.)

You can use user parameters to automatically fill in whatever fields make sense for your job. You can change or delete any of these settings at any time.

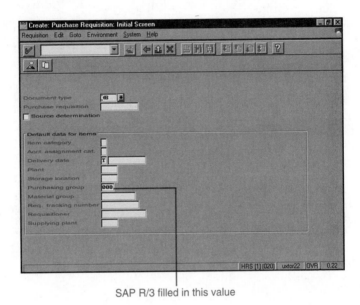

SAP R/3 filled in this value

FIGURE 16.4   The value 8 is the user parameter for this field.

In this lesson, you learned how to use user parameters to cut
down on the typing you need to do when creating new business
documents. In the next lesson, you learn how to use User Menus
to provide custom access paths.

Using User Menus

In this lesson, you learn how to use user menus to provide custom access paths.

What You Need for This Lesson

For this lesson, you need access to several SAP submenus so that you can set up your own access paths.

 Access Paths The sequence of menus and menu commands you need to select to get to a screen.

Setting Up a User Menu

A user menu allows you to set up direct access paths to those parts of the system that you use the most frequently. If most of your work is buried deep in several levels of menus, this will simplify your way of getting to it.

Follow these steps to set up a custom menu:

1. From any screen, select System, User Profile, Start User Menu. The User Menu dialog box shown in Figure 17.1 appears.

2. Place the cursor on your User ID and click the Configure button. An empty user menu appears.

3. Click the New Entries button, and SAP R/3 displays a dialog box in which you are to supply a name for this menu area (see Figure 17.2).

FIGURE 17.1   Starting a new user menu.

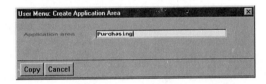

FIGURE 17.2   You can use any name that suits the way you work.

4. Enter a name for your new area, such as Purchasing.

5. Next you have to tell SAP which of its standard menu choices you want to copy to your own user menu. Click the Copy button, and the structure of the standard SAP R/3 menu appears (see Figure 17.3).

6. A plus sign in front of an entry means that it contains sub-entries. Open up successive levels by clicking the plus signs until you get down to the function you would like to add. Select an item and click Copy. The User Menu: Change Text dialog box appears (see Figure 17.4).

7. **(Optional)** SAP R/3 already has a name for the menu item. However, you can change how it appears on your custom menu, naming it anything you want. (For example, you might use the name Create Vendor known, as shown in Figure 17.4.)

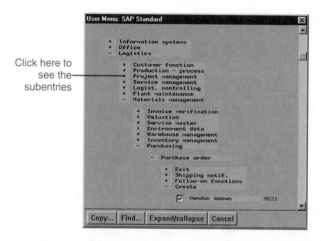

Click here to
see the
subentries

FIGURE 17.3   Click a selection box to choose an item.

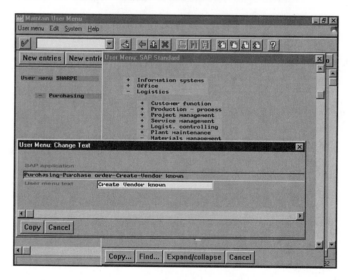

FIGURE 17.4   How do you want it to appear on your menu?

8. Click Copy, and SAP R/3 adds one area (Purchasing) to
   your user menu, as well as one item (Create Vendor
   known) under it. Repeat steps 6–8 to create a structure
   like the one shown in Figure 17.5.

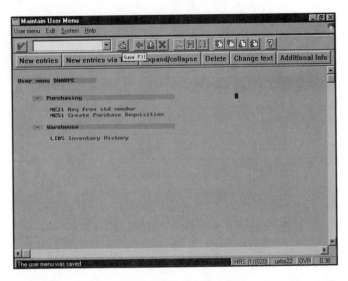

FIGURE 17.5   The structure of your new menus.

9. Click Save to save your new menu. Then click the Back
   toolbutton to return to the previous screen.

To activate your user menu again, you must log off and then log
back on again. When you do, you'll see that the User Menu dialog
box shows the names of the areas and the menu choices you
specified (see Figure 17.6).

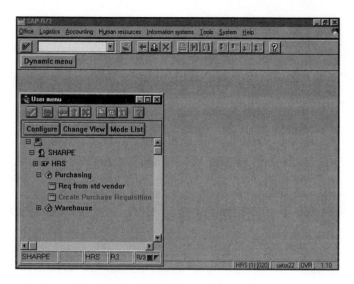

FIGURE 17.6   Your finished menu.

You can open and close branches by clicking the plus and minus signs, and you can make a selection by double-clicking an item.

In this lesson, you learned how to create and use your own menus. In the next lesson, you will learn how to bypass the menus completely by using transaction codes and how to run and move between multiple sessions of SAP R/3.

18 Using Transaction Codes

In this lesson, you will learn how to bypass the menus by using transaction codes and how to look up the transaction codes for screens to which you know the menu path. You will also learn how to run and move between multiple sessions of SAP R/3.

What You Need for This Lesson

For this lesson, you will need one of the following:

- A User ID with authority to display purchase requisitions

- A User ID with authority to display another transaction so you can follow along

Getting Directly to a Transaction

Every SAP R/3 screen has a transaction code. You might find it helpful to jump right into a screen to check a value such as a price or a stock level.

 Transaction Code A shortcut that takes you directly into the SAP R/3 screen that begins a particular transaction.

Here is how you use a transaction code to go to a particular screen and find the information you need.

1. From the first SAP R/3 screen, move your cursor to the command field by clicking there (see Figure 18.1).

Command field

FIGURE 18.1   Enter the transaction code in the command field.

2. Type **/n** followed by the transaction code, and press Enter. For this example, type **/nme52** in the command
   field. (I'll explain the reason for "/n" later in this lesson;
   note, however, that the slash is a forward slash, not a
   back slash.) Because me52 is the transaction code for the
   Change: Purchase Requisition screen, the Create Purchase
   Requisition: Initial Screen appears.

Some users find it convenient to use transaction codes to move
directly to a screen instead of using the menus. Although experienced users often use transaction codes, you shouldn't use them
when you're learning SAP R/3; menus are a less intimidating way
to learn the system.

Should You Use Them?   Although they're sometimes
convenient, transaction codes are a throwback to the "old
days" in computing, when you had to memorize lists of
cryptic commands. The problem is, if you only know how
to get to a screen by using transaction codes and you
forget a transaction code, you won't know how to find
your way back to that screen!

FINDING A TRANSACTION CODE

Once you're comfortable with SAP, you may find that you prefer
using transaction codes to get around. But suppose you don't
know the transaction code for a screen you need to access. No
problem. You can find the transaction code for any screen your
system uses. Here's how:

1. Go to the screen for which you want to find the transaction code.

2. Choose System, Status. SAP displays the System: Status screen shown in Figure 18.2.

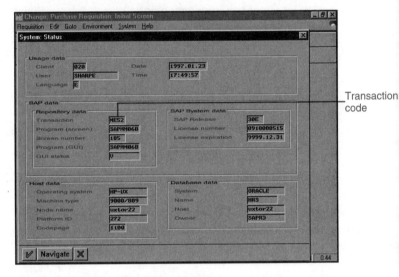

Transaction code

Figure 18.2 The System: Status screen.

3. You'll find the transaction code clearly labeled here; in this case, it's ME52. If you want to, write down the transaction code for future reference.

TIP

Transaction, Not Screen The transaction code is not really specific to a *screen*, but to a *transaction*. An example of a transaction is Create Purchase Requisition, which may include several screens. If several screens are required to complete a transaction, entering the code will simply take you to the first one.

USING TRANSACTION CODES TO OPEN A NEW SESSION

At the beginning of this lesson, you typed **/nme52** in the command field. But you knew only that ME52 was the actual transaction code. So what does the /n in the command field do?

The /n prefix tells SAP *how* you want it to use the transaction code. There are two ways of using a transaction code: you indicate which you want by preceding the transaction code with /n or /o, as explained here:

- **/n** tells SAP that you want it to abandon the screen you are currently on and move to a new screen, which is identified by this transaction code.

- **/o** tells SAP that you want to go to a new screen identified by the transaction code, but that you want your original *session* to remain open. (So you can have two open sessions.) To try this method, from the main SAP R/3 screen, type **/ome52** (o as in orange). The same Change: Purchase Requisition: Initial screen appears—on top of the previous screen (see Figure 18.3).

Session   A session is an independent job running in its own window. You can have several sessions open at once.

Why is having more than one session open important? Sometimes when you are midway through one transaction, you need to check something in another part of the system. For example, suppose you are creating a Requisition, and you want to check something on the Vendor master. If you know the transaction code for displaying the Vendor master, you can open a second session but keep the first one open.

Window to full screen control

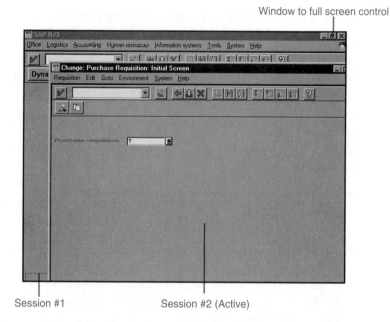

Session #1   Session #2 (Active)

FIGURE 18.3   You can have two sessions open on the desktop at once.

When you have more than one session open, you need to know how to move back and forth between them. You can use the Window to full screen control in the upper-right corner of your window to make both sessions visible at the same time, as shown in Figure 18.3. Then you just click in the session you want to work in to make it active. Alternatively, you can press Alt+Tab to display a list of the open sessions (see Figure 18.4). Then you select the session you want to move to (just as you do to move between other Windows 95 sessions).

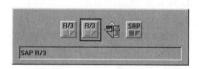

FIGURE 18.4   Moving between sessions with Alt+Tab.

ANOTHER WAY TO OPEN A NEW SESSION

Sometimes you may want to open another session, but you might not know the transaction code you need to get there. You can start another session from any screen by choosing System, Create Session. SAP opens a new session that starts at the initial SAP R/3 screen. Then you can use the menus to navigate to where you want to be.

You can close any session by clicking the Close (X) button or by repeatedly clicking the Exit toolbutton.

I Can Do That from the Desktop   Of course, you could just open another session from the Windows desktop by clicking the icon you used to launch SAP R/3 in the first place. But if you do that, you have to log on again with your User ID and password. It is much easier to create a new session from within SAP R/3.

In this lesson, you learned how to find and use transaction codes. You also learned how to open and close new sessions and how to move between them. In the next lesson, you will learn how to customize your User ID.

19 CUSTOMIZING YOUR USER ID

In this lesson, you will learn how to change the settings for your User ID.

SETTING THE DEFAULTS

A *default* is a certain value that SAP R/3 uses every time it encounters a particular field, unless you specifically give it another value. You can specify what you want the default for a field to be.

The following steps walk you through setting your user default values:

1. From any screen, choose System, User Profile, User Defaults. The Maintain User: Defaults screen appears (see Figure 19.1). Note the following elements of this screen:

   - The User field is just your user logon name, or User ID.

   - The Start Menu field enables you to set up a menu for R/3 to start off with when you log on. For example, if you enter ME00 in this field, you would automatically go to the Purchasing screen every time you log on. (To learn how to find the codes for other screens, see Lesson 18, "Using Transaction Codes.")

   - The Output Device is the printer that SAP R/3 will use for your reports. Remember, though, that you can always redirect your job to another printer at the time of printing by typing another value over the default. (Some SAP R/3 documents may print to a predefined printer; for example, your Purchase Orders might always be sent to a printer in Purchasing. Changing the default here will not change the destinations for such predefined documents.)

Getting Help   Remember that you can always use the SAP R/3 Field Level Help to learn more about how to use the fields.

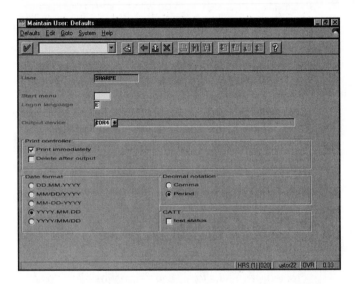

FIGURE 19.1   Change your user defaults from this screen.

2. Move your cursor to the Output Device field and click the matchcode arrow. (If a Restrict Value Ranges box appears, just click No.) SAP displays a list of all the printers that are defined to the SAP R/3 system to which you are connected. Scroll through the list and find the printer you want to use. Double-click an item to select it.

3. In the Print Controller area, select both Print Immediately and Delete After Printing for normal use. (Again, you can override these defaults at the time of printing if you want to.)

4. Select the default date format you will use to enter dates when working in SAP, and choose your preference for the decimal notation. You must enter all dates in SAP R/3 in the format you select here. If you don't, SAP will not

accept your entries. Similarly, you must also use the decimal notation you indicate here.

Date Format   The format you use to enter all dates is set here. It has nothing to do with how SAP R/3 stores dates internally, just with how they are displayed and entered for *your* User ID.

5. The CATT test status control is used only for Computer Assisted Testing. Leave it as is.

6. Click Save to save your changes, and then click the Back toolbutton to return to the previous screen.

Keep It Simple   In practice, it is a good idea to define a standard date presentation for your organization. (Somebody may have already done this where you work.) For training, it is certainly better to stick to one way of presenting and entering dates. Much unnecessary confusion is created when date formats in training materials do not match the format of a new user's ID.

CUSTOMIZING WINDOW AND CURSOR

Another menu is provided to change your window and cursor control. It is tucked away in the upper-right corner and is easy to forget. If you can't remember where to find the settings for controlling a default option, check under this icon:

1. From any SAP R/3 screen, click this icon (located at the right end of the menu bar).

2. From the pull-down menu that appears, choose Options. The Options dialog box appears (see Figure 19.2).

FIGURE 19.2   The Options dialog box.

3. Select the General tab if it is not already selected. There you will find the following options:

- You can turn off the toolbars or the status bar, but short of mean practical jokes, I can't imagine why you would want to.

- The Quick Info options control how quickly the little helper boxes appear when you move your cursor to an item.

- You can specify how SAP warns you of messages. If no boxes are checked, SAP R/3 gives you error and abort messages on a discreet little line at the bottom of the screen (as you have seen so far). However, you can have them displayed as an in-your-face dialog box, and you can also have SAP R/3 beep to wake you up.

- The System Libraries option sets how parts of R/3 are used. (Your tech support people can tell you how it is usually set in your company; you probably won't ever have to change this.)

4. Click the Colors in Forms or Colors in Lists tab (shown in Figure 19.3) to adjust your colors. You can change any of these settings to suit your preferences. These colors are stored with your User ID and will be in effect no matter what machine you log on with.

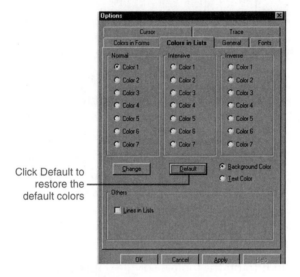

Click Default to restore the default colors

FIGURE 19.3   The Colors in Lists tab.

TIP   **For the Aesthetically Challenged**   If you have changed the color settings around and don't like (or can't read) the results, you can fix them. For Forms, return the Color Palettes setting to Standard. For Colors in Lists, click Default to restore the colors.

5. Explore the other options available on the Cursor, Fonts, and Trace tabs. However, before you make any changes to them, write down the original settings. They do not provide those convenient Default buttons that return the settings to how they started.

Screen Fonts These fonts have nothing to do with the way SAP R/3 prints information on paper; they only affect how text appears on your screen.

6. Click OK to close this dialog box, and SAP R/3 saves your changes.

Customizing Your Screen Size

You can customize your screen size using either of two methods: You can change the number of dots your Windows desktop can display, or you can change the default size that SAP R/3 uses for your User ID.

The first method really affects a Windows 95 setting. Any change you make to the Windows desktop settings applies to your computer, *not* your User ID. The SAP R/3 data entry screens are all planned around "lowest common denominator" settings (640 dots wide by 480 dots high). If a data-entry screen had more information than would fit on a 640×480 screen, the SAP designers would break it out into several screens or provided scroll bars.

Many PCs now are able to display higher resolution screens at 600×800, or 768×1,024, or even higher. You can control your setting through Windows if your PC hardware supports it.

There are two reasons you might want to go to a higher resolution:

- For reports and lists, you can get a wider and longer viewing space, which means you can see more items on a list. You can drag the SAP R/3 window open to a larger size.

- If your work involves having several SAP R/3 sessions open at once, you can have several overlapping 640×480 sessions open on your larger desktop.

The downside is that the higher resolution you use on your monitor, the smaller the text becomes.

To change your Windows 95 to a higher resolution, follow these steps:

1. Click the Start button, choose Settings, and choose Control Panel.

2. In the Control Panel window, choose Display.

3. In the Display Properties dialog box, choose Settings, and the Settings tab of the Display Properties dialog box appears (see Figure 19.4).

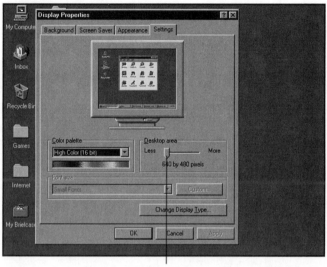

If there is room to the right of this slider, you can try a higher resolution

Figure 19.4   Change your Windows 95 screen settings from here.

4. Move the slider to the resolution you want. Depending on your computer, going to a higher resolution may cause the Color Palette to change, too. This is limited by the amount of memory on your video card.

5. Click OK to put your new settings into effect.

Don't Be Hasty   Sometimes when you change your screen resolution, it causes problems displaying the screen at the new resolution. Windows 95 gets around this problem by changing the resolution, and then putting a message on the screen asking if you want to keep the settings. If you click Yes, you must have been able to read the message. If you don't do anything for 15 seconds, Windows thinks "Oh no, the human can't read the screen. I'll change it back." So, if there is a problem, don't do anything precipitous—just sit back and wait a minute.

As I said, there are two ways you can customize your screen size. The second is under SAP R/3 and applies to your User ID.

You can customize the default window size that SAP R/3 uses to display your screens by clicking the Display Options icon and selecting Default Size. If you have Windows 95 set up for a resolution of 640×480 (as shown in Figure 19.4), this setting will have no effect.

In this lesson, you learned how to customize the defaults and settings for your window, cursor, colors, and fonts for your User ID. You also learned that SAP R/3 can take advantage of a larger Windows 95 desktop and how to create one on your PC. In the next lesson, you will learn what configuration is and how it affects you.

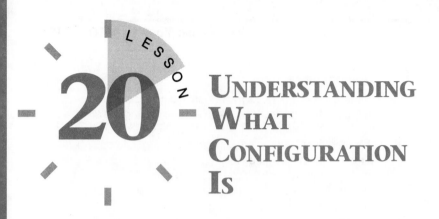

20 LESSON UNDERSTANDING WHAT CONFIGURATION IS

In this lesson, you will learn what configuration is and how it affects you as a user.

CONFIGURATION: ADAPTING TO YOUR SPECIFIC REQUIREMENTS

Most organizations have developed their own ways of conducting internal business to suit their products, services, markets, and organizational "style." SAP R/3 was designed to allow each organization to adapt how the system works in the same way—to fit its own needs.

The next section will discuss how *configuration*, the process of adjusting SAP R/3 to your specifications, can make your SAP R/3 program match the way you do business.

CONFIGURATION AND CHANGE: AN INEVITABLE COMBINATION

Changing the way you do business is often a big part of the SAP R/3 equation, and the process of change usually begins right away. Sometimes business methods are not well documented within an organization, and sometimes they are understood differently by different departments. Therefore, when your organization begins using SAP R/3, the first thing to do is to determine and document how various departments work together.

The first aspect of configuration normally involves assembling department experts into an SAP R/3 implementation team. These experts (and usually some SAP R/3 consultants) document how things are done in your company. Doing a good job here is critical to the success of any SAP R/3 project.

Next, the implementation team decides whether the existing business processes should be modified. In many cases, the process of documenting and reviewing how an organization does business produces many important ideas for improvement. If the implementation team decides to make changes in addition to installing SAP R/3 (most companies do make some changes), it has the following options:

- Change the business process first and then implement SAP R/3 with the new processes

- Implement SAP R/3 with the old business process and change the process later

- Implement SAP R/3 and change the business process at the same time

Note, however, that these are not mutually exclusive choices; companies usually choose a combination.

MOVING WITH THE CHANGES

An organization normally starts with a plain vanilla copy of SAP R/3 set up for a generic company (see Lesson 23 for exceptions). Configuration is the process of adapting this vanilla copy to your business.

Given the number of complex interactions that a company experiences every day, there will inevitably be configuration changes up to, during, and after implementation of your SAP R/3 system.

Reactive or Proactive?   In a perfect organization, all configuration changes would be proactive. You see the need for changes and make them before any problems surface. In the real world, there will be unforeseen problems that necessitate reactive changes to the configuration. These difficulties are normal and usually can be quickly dealt with.

Whatever the reason behind it, configuration change is normal for any implementation. Don't be alarmed if something that works one way today works a little differently tomorrow. Here are some configuration issues that you should be aware of:

- **Don't be afraid of change.** Your SAP R/3 configuration will change most significantly before and during implementation. After that, it will continue to change when your company makes business process changes, when a new release of SAP R/3 offers a better approach for your business, and when your company is reorganized.

- **The are several kinds of changes.** A business process change could be, for example, changing the way Purchase Orders are approved. An organizational change might be, say, splitting the Materials Management group across your divisions. Either move could call for configuration changes.

- **Did you find a problem?** Don't be surprised if you are the one to discover a need for configuration changes. It is nearly impossible for the implementation team to consider all the possible variations of business processes and their interactions with the SAP R/3 program.

WHAT ABOUT THINGS SAP R/3 DOESN'T DO?

In most businesses, you can find specialized tasks that a general solution such as SAP R/3 does not address. When you find such tasks, you can handle it in either of two ways:

- By writing custom extensions to SAP R/3

- By using another commercially available solution and interfacing it to your SAP R/3 system

Many companies write extensions or changes to their SAP R/3 programs to accommodate unique ways of doing business. These alterations are written in a programming language called ABAP.

ABAP   The computer language that SAP R/3 is written in. This is normally the language your company would use for writing extensions to SAP R/3.

While custom extensions can be helpful, there are some potential shortcomings:

- The more you write yourself, the more you start to lose the advantages of buying a software package.

- The built-in SAP R/3 Help systems won't provide you with any assistance on custom programs developed for your company. Your company will have to provide manuals, training, or online help for those extensions.

- The more customization that is done, the harder it is to move to new releases of SAP R/3 software.

Specialized Systems   There are some highly specialized systems that most businesses will need to keep, even after they have implemented SAP R/3. Many companies writing these kinds of systems are working to make them easy to interface with SAP R/3. SAP R/3 does not aim to replace all business systems, just the core ones that are common to most organizations.

In this lesson, you learned what configuration is and how it affects you. You also (hopefully) learned that change is normal before, during, and after implementation. In the next lesson, you will learn about SAP R/3 and the Internet.

21 SAP R/3 AND THE INTERNET

In this lesson, you learn how SAP R/3 will facilitate business on the Internet. You will also get a look at SAP's home page on the World Wide Web.

DOING BUSINESS ON THE WEB WITH SAP R/3

SAP has developed ways R/3 (and even its predecessor, R/2) can be used with the Internet. Version 3.1 is the Java-enabled version of R/3.

> **Java** Java is a programming language. Think of Java as an extension to your Web browser (Netscape or Internet Explorer). With Java, small programs are sent to you that automatically run inside your browser. Programs written in Java will run on any browser that supports it, regardless of whether the browser is running on a Windows PC, a Mac, or a network computer.

In conjunction with Microsoft, SAP has developed technologies that create numerous possibilities, including the following:

- Connection of a remote user to a central R/3 system through the Internet. The programs that present the SAP R/3 front end to you are Java programs running inside your browser. Your SAP R/3 screens are displayed in your Netscape or Internet Explorer windows. This will make it easier to distribute SAP R/3 geographically where there are no traditional LANs or WANs in place.

LAN and WAN   Local area network and wide area network. These are the kinds of networks used by most businesses to connect their in-house desktop computers.

- Communication of ALE (Application Link Enabling) messages through the Internet.

ALE   Application Link Enabling defines standards for coupling SAP R/3 components running in different locations. It is used for things such as consolidating sales data from independent SAP R/3 systems and updating master files on remote systems. ALE messages can be SAP R/3 to SAP R/3 or SAP to other products.

- Customer ordering/payment interface. It will be possible, through specially designed interfaces, for customers to create their orders directly on your SAP R/3 system via the Internet. The necessary controls will, of course, be available.

- Customer quotation/information interface. Customers will be able to get product and pricing information through the Internet.

- Defined outside access to R/3 applications. You will be able to give your customers immediate access to information regarding their orders, accounts, deliveries, and so on.

- Move data entry out to the point of capture (the place where the information is created). For example, suppose you run a network of retail outlets. You could have the managers directly input the "closing data" every night instead of sending in forms. (You could set up special interfaces to SAP R/3 for these employees, so all they would need to know is the point-and-click stuff, not the whole SAP R/3 interface.)

VISITING SAP'S HOME PAGE ON THE WORLD WIDE WEB

The Internet is one area where SAP is moving very quickly. To see what they have developed or are planning this month, you should check out their home page on the Net.

If you have access to a World Wide Web browser (such as Netscape or Microsoft Internet Explorer), you can visit SAP on their home page located at **http://www.sap.com/**. The SAP home page, shown in Figure 21.1, is a great source of information about what's new with SAP. Newsletters, technical articles, press releases, and other useful information can all be found there.

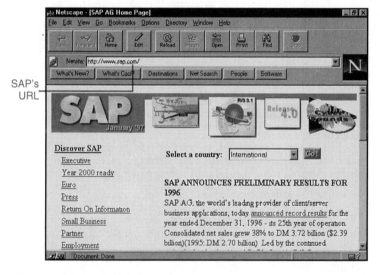

FIGURE 21.1   SAP's home page, as it appeared January, 1997.

URL (Uniform Resource Locator)   This is the "address" of a Web page. Every page on the World Wide Web has its own URL.

It's Not the Same! If the page on your screen doesn't look like this one, don't worry—you're still in the right place. The appearance of the SAP page varies from month to month. (Their URL stays the same, though.)

Most of the documents available for download from the SAP page are in Adobe Acrobat format. The *extension* (the last three characters of the file name) for files in this format is .PDF.

Like a magazine, this format is great for printing mixed text and graphics, but the files are usually rather large and take a few minutes to download. In order to read the .PDF files, you need to download the Adobe Acrobat reader from the Web; you can find it at **http://www.adobe.com/acrobat/**.

If you decide to print these documents after you download them, note that it can take a long time and use up (temporarily) loads of disk space during printing. On the other hand, browsing them on your screen with the Adobe Acrobat reader is quick and fairly easy. The SAP home page suggests a way that you can download all the PDFs from an issue of their magazine into a directory, where you can read it as a single online magazine. Click Helper Applications to find out more about it.

Reading the Newsgroup

UseNet is like a huge discussion group that is broken down into thousands of areas called *newsgroups*. You can find a newsgroup on every topic imaginable, from home brewing to astronomy—and among them is a newsgroup for SAP R/3. People post messages every day to share thoughts, ideas, and questions about SAP R/3 with other interested parties.

If you have a newsreader and your Internet service provider includes a news server, you can read or subscribe to the SAP R/3 newsgroup. Figure 21.2 shows WinVN, which is an example of a dedicated newsreader. Both the Netscape Navigator and Internet Explorer browsers also contain newsreaders with which you can read newsgroups.

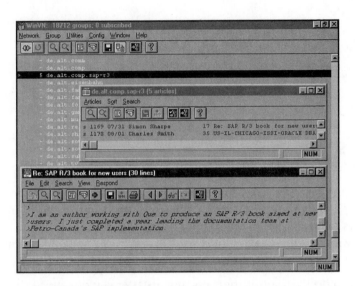

FIGURE 21.2   Cruising the SAP R/3 newsgroup with WinVN.

The newsgroup name is **de.alt.comp.sap-r3**. The "de" stands for Deutsch and is used because SAP is a German company. Most "de" newsgroups are in German; however, most of the news in this particular group is in English.

This newsgroup is not sponsored or officially supported by SAP. It is just an open forum for people involved in setting up and using SAP R/3. As you'll see, a lot of the postings seem to be posted by people looking for work or companies looking for people. There is some technical and organizational information also. As in any newsgroup, you can post your own observations or questions here if you want.

In this lesson, you learned about SAP's plans for using R/3 with the Internet. You also learned about the SAP home page and the UseNet newsgroup. In the next lesson, you will learn about the different kinds of SAP R/3 business documents and how they are used.

KINDS OF BUSINESS DOCUMENTS

In this lesson, you will learn the purpose of some common types of documents used in SAP R/3.

KINDS OF BUSINESS DOCUMENTS

In very general terms, there are two kinds of data in any system:

- **Master data** This data is relatively fixed in your system. Your company could continue to run for days without creating new master data. Not all master data has the word "master" in its name. Customer Master, Personnel Master, and Chart of Accounts are all examples of master data. (These are discussed in more detail in Lesson 15, "Using Master Data.")

- **Transaction data** This data is made up of the normal day-to-day business transactions in a system. If you couldn't create these documents, your business would come to a stop. Purchase Orders, Invoices, and Production Orders are all examples of transaction data.

  With *transaction data*, there is usually a chain of documents involved in any process. For example, a document may start as an inquiry from a customer, be converted into a quotation, and then work its way through the system to finally become an invoice and a payment.

It is important to know where the documents you work with come from and go to so that you understand the implications of any errors or problems that might be found in the document.

Table 22.1 lists the common SAP R/3 documents and their purpose, as well as the R/3 modules that use the information, its predecessor, and some subsequent documents.

For each kind of document, there are variations in how it can be created or processed. For example, a Purchase Order could be created from scratch, from a Requisition, from the MRP process, and so on.

This Is Not a Definitive List   Many documents and relationships in SAP R/3 are not included in this list. As of February 1997, SAP R/3's Business Object Repository lists 170 different kinds of business objects. (An example of a business object would be a Purchase Order.) Although this list is not comprehensive, it covers the most common objects.

TABLE 22.1   THE MOST COMMON SAP R/3 DOCUMENTS

NAME	DESCRIPTION	USED BY	PREDECESSORS	SUBSEQUENT
Bill of Materials	Lists items needed to build a product	PP		
Credit Memo	Tells the customer their account has been credited	SD, FI		
Customer Payment	Records receipt of payment from customer	FI	Invoice	
Debit Memo	Tells the customer their account has been debited	SD, FI	Invoice	
Delivery	Records delivery of goods	SD	Sales Order	

NAME	DESCRIPTION	USED BY	PREDECESSORS	SUBSEQUENT
Delivery, free of charge	Records delivery of samples or items for complaint resolution	SD	Inquiry	
Goods Issue	Authorizes goods removed from stock	MM, PP, SD		
Goods Receipt	Records receipt of goods from external supplier	MM, QM	Purchase Order	
Inquiries	Customer request for information	SD		Quotation
Inspection Lot	Request for inspection	QM		
Invoice (1)	Request for payment sent to a customer	SD, FI	Sales Order	
Invoice (2)	Request for payment received from a vendor	FI	Purchase Order	
Maintenance Notification	Request for maintenance	PM		
Maintenance Order	Order authorizing service	PM, CO	Maintenance Notification	
Material Reservation	Reserves a material that is in stock	PP, SD, PM		
Order Proposal	Proposed order for your stock or production	MM (MRP)		
Outline Agreement (1)	Documents terms agreed with customer for use over a specified time period	SD		Release Order (theirs)

continues

Table 22.1   Continued

Name	Description	Used By	Predecessors	Subsequent
Outline Agreement (2)	Documents terms agreed with vendor for use over a specified time period	MM		Release Order (yours)
Picking List	List of materials to be removed from stock	MM		
Pricing and Condition	Prices, discounts surcharges, and so on	SD		Sales Orders
Production Order	Schedule of production of goods	PP, QM	Sales Order, Planned Order, Production Proposal	Delivery
Planned Order	Production slot reserved to fill a customer's order	MM (MRP)	Sales Order	Purchase Requisition
Purchase Order	Order for goods or services from a vendor	MM, FI, QM	Purchase Requisition	Goods Receipt
Purchase Requisition	Request to MM from business unit for goods or services	MM	Plan Order	Purchase Order
Q-Info Record	Vendor's status (blocked, allowed) for a material	QM	Quality Assurance Agreement	
Quality Assurance Agreement	Agreement with vendor that allows procurement of a given material	QM		Q-Info Record
Quotation	Offer to supply goods and materials at specified terms	SD	Inquiry	Sales Order

NAME	**DESCRIPTION**	**USED BY**	**PREDECESSORS**	**SUBSEQUENT**
Release Order	Used with out-line agreement to request product	MM	Outline Agreement	
Return	Records customer number, date, reason, and so on	SD	Delivery	
RFQ	Records product amount, vendor, and so on	MM	Purchase Order	
Sales Order	Records customer number, date, line-items	SD, MM, FI	Quotation	Delivery, Invoice
Time Tickets	Shop floor paper for worker to fill in the time an operation took	PP, FI, HR, PM		

In this lesson, you learned about the most common documents, that documents are often shared between SAP R/3 modules, and that most documents either trigger subsequent documents or are triggered by earlier documents. In the next lesson, you will learn what the industry solutions are and how they may affect you.

SAP R/3 INDUSTRY SOLUTIONS

In this lesson, you learn what the Industry Solutions are and how they may affect you.

WHAT IS AN INDUSTRY SOLUTION?

A generic copy of SAP R/3 provides a starting point for most businesses. However, some companies (because of the nature of their business) can benefit from starting with a version of SAP R/3 that has been customized for their industry. Such versions are called Industry Solutions.

The Industry Solutions versions of SAP are different from the vanilla SAP R/3 because they are (somewhat) preconfigured and have *extensions*. This does not mean your company can bypass the configuration step, but it does mean a better fit between your "out-of-the-box" system and your needs.

 Extensions Additions to SAP R/3 that do not come with the plain version. They are programs that are written to add industry-specific functionality to R/3.

In essence, the Industry Solutions give you the benefit of the learnings and experience from earlier SAP R/3 installations in your industry.

EXAMPLES OF INDUSTRY SOLUTIONS

The Industry Solutions available now include the following:

> **IS-A (Administration)** This Industry Solution is geared towards fiscal accounting and budget management.

IS-B (Banking)   This is geared toward financial institutions.

IS-H (Hospital)   This is designed for hospital administration.

IS-IS (Insurance)   This is for insurance companies and financial service providers. It helps manage securities and loans.

IS-Oil   This is designed for the oil industry.

IS-PI (Process Industry)   This provides control and production planning for process industries. (A chemical plant is an example of a process industry.)

IS-P (Publishing)   This is aimed at periodical publishers.

How Industry Solutions Affect You

If you start from an Industry Solution, your configuration time will probably be shorter, and configuration will present fewer risks than if you were to start with generic SAP R/3. You also might need to adapt your business processes less than you would with a generic version.

Some kinds of industries do not yet have Industry Solutions. It is possible that your business will first implement SAP R/3 using a generic version that has been configured for your company, and later switch to an Industry Solution-based system. This would likely be another large project, similar to (but hopefully easier than) your original SAP R/3 implementation.

Industry Solutions and the Future

As SAP R/3 continues to develop, it is likely that more Industry Solutions will become available. These solutions should become more detailed and better tuned to their respective industries as people work with them and see opportunities for increased efficiency.

Here's a glimpse of what the future might hold for SAP R/3:

- SAP is planning to decouple SAP R/3 so that companies can buy and implement only the modules they need.

- SAP R/3 will be soon be used by many medium-sized businesses, in addition to the large corporations that are using it now. Although this integration will cost them money up front, it will help not only their internal integration, but also their integration with other companies using SAP R/3.

- Because of SAP R/3's integration capabilities, more companies will be willing to outsource services (using SAP R/3 to integrate the functions) that they might not consider outsourcable today.

Outsource The current euphemism for contacting services to farm out functions that were formerly done by in-house staff.

The primary benefit of SAP R/3 is its quick efficiency in business information processing. Some people feel the Internet performs (or will perform) this function just as well and don't see a need to implement SAP R/3. Although it is true that the Net can help you get more life out of your existing systems, R/3 offers much more to business process integration than just the capability to send data between systems.

In this lesson, you learned about Industry Solutions and how they could affect you. You also learned about some future possibilities involving SAP R/3 and Industry Solutions. In the appendixes, you will get a small taste of what is in the various SAP R/3 modules, as well as an idea of how the modules work together.

Sales and Distribution, Materials Management, and Production Planning Modules

 Wait! Before you read this appendix, be sure you are familiar with the different kinds of SAP R/3 business documents explained in Lesson 22.

Sales and Distribution

Sales and Distribution (SD) includes the business processes used to sell and deliver products and services to customers and business partners. Information about the products and customers (both of which are stored as master data) is used in SD.

To handle these business processes, the structure of your company needs to be represented in SAP R/3.

For example, if you have a Head Office and several Sales Organizations (classed by region or by product, for example), the Head Office could be represented with a Client Code, and the Sales Organizations could be indicated by Company Codes. Your Sales Organizations could be broken down further into Distribution Channels. You might also have a *matrix* organization where different Divisions exist for different products. And finally, you could have Sales areas where the matrices cross. Figure A.1 illustrates this type of structure.

Matrix   A matrix organization exists when a subgroup in a company belongs to more than one group.

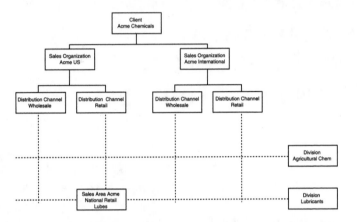

Figure A.1   One way a complex company could be represented for SD in SAP R/3.

Divisions   Your organization might not use all of these divisions, or it might use them a little differently. The point is that the structure of your company needs to be accurately represented in SAP R/3 in order for the system to correctly process sales information.

To get a flavor for SD, follow a typical sale through the system. There are many other ways you could process a sale.

The following list outlines functions and benefits of SAP R/3's SD module:

- SD adapts to various scenarios: A customer might simply call and place an order, or there might be an existing Contract or Scheduling Agreement with a customer that predefines price and delivery.

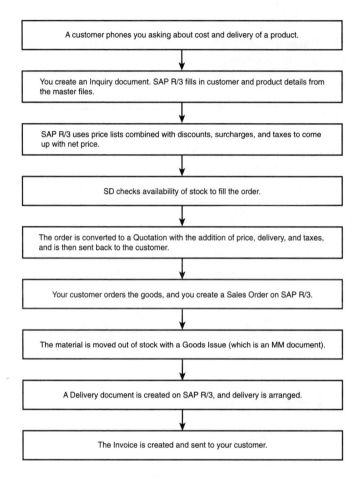

- You can price orders manually.

- SD provides for the processing of exceptions such as returns and free deliveries.

- You can create a Sales Order with reference to a Quotation, and all the appropriate values from the Quotation will be copied into the Sales Order.

The main documents used in SD include the Sales Order, Inquiry, Quotation, Outline Agreement (contract and scheduling), Return, No Charge Delivery, Delivery, Debit Memo, Credit Memo, and *Info Record*. The main master files used by SD are Customer Master, Material Master, and Inventory Master.

> **Info Record** An Info Record combines customer and product information. It lists things specific to a certain product for a certain customer. For example, you could use an Info Record to track your customer's product number.

SD reports the quantities to MM to ensure that stock is reserved or ordered. SD also forwards billing information to FI for credit checks and receivables postings.

MATERIALS MANAGEMENT

Materials Management (MM) includes the business processes used for purchasing, material requirement planning, goods receipt, and inventory management. Materials Management has a strong connection with SD; for instance, your company's MM department will be dealing with other companies' SD departments and vice versa.

The structure of your company also needs to be represented in SAP R/3 for MM. Figure A.2 shows a typical way you might represent your purchasing organization.

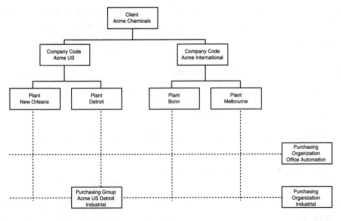

FIGURE A.2   One way a complex purchasing structure could be represented in SAP R/3.

As with SD, the top level is Client, which is normally used to represent your head office. Within Client, your organization can be subdivided into Company code and then Purchasing Group. A matrix can be used if you have central groups responsible for the purchase of a certain class of materials. Again, your company might not need to use all of these divisions, or it might use them differently.

The following flow chart illustrates a typical component for buying, assembly, and selling, thereby showing you how MM functions.

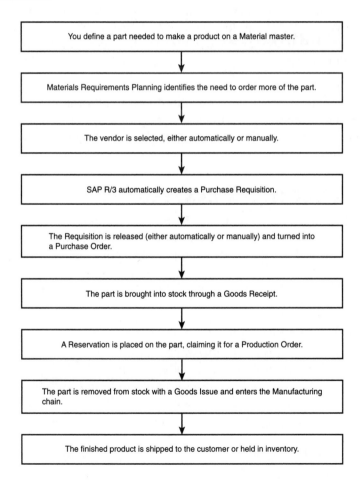

MRP can generate proposed orders based on order point, order quantity, Sales Orders from SD, reservations on existing stock, and so on.

Availability   Just because you see an item on the shelf doesn't mean it is available. It could have a Material Reservation against it. If you really want to know what's available, check SAP R/3, not the shelf.

The main documents used in MM are the Purchase Requisition, Purchase Order, Goods Receipt, and Goods Issue. The main master files used in MM are Material Master, Inventory Master, and Vendor Master.

Purchasing passes information to Controlling (CO) so that CO can assign costs to the appropriate cost center. Purchasing shares the Vendor master with Financial Accounting (FI). Purchasing takes information from SD to perform Material Requirements Planning.

PRODUCTION PLANNING

Production Planning (PP) includes the business processes used to plan and figure the cost of production orders. The company structure reflected in PP starts at the top with Client number, which represents your head office. The Company code is next, followed by the units, which are subdivided into Plants and Work Centers (see Figure A.3).

Bill of Materials (BOM), Routing   Making an analogy to a recipe, the Bill of Materials is the ingredients list, and the Routing is the instructions.

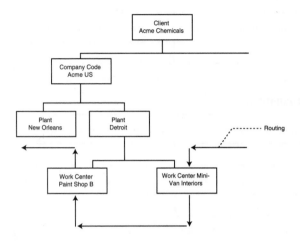

FIGURE A.3 One way of representing a production organization in SAP R/3. Part of a *Routing* is shown.

To get a quick overview of Production Planning, follow the sample production run shown in the following flow chart.

PP also handles the following functions:

- Scheduling of Production Resources & Tools and Capacity Leveling.

- Make-to-Order (job-shop) and Repetitive Manufacturing (make-for-stock) jobs.

- External processing, where your product receives some processing at an outside company.

- Directing the printing of shop floor notices to the appropriate shop-floor printer.

The main documents used in PP include Production Order, Bill of Material, Material Provision List, Goods Reservation, Completion Confirmation, Time Ticket, Production Resource & Tools Overviews, and Withdrawal Slip. The main master files used in PP include Routings, Work Centers, and Material Master.

PP interfaces with MM, Human Resources (HR), and CO.

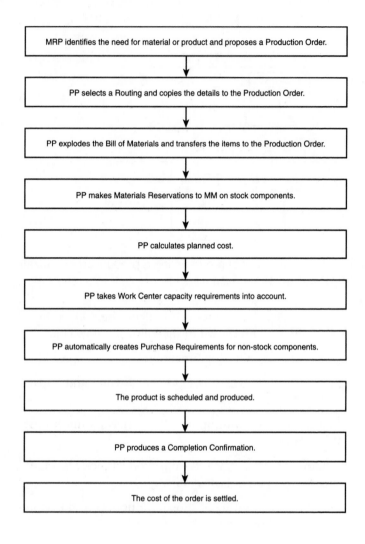

MRP identifies the need for material or product and proposes a Production Order.

PP selects a Routing and copies the details to the Production Order.

PP explodes the Bill of Materials and transfers the items to the Production Order.

PP makes Materials Reservations to MM on stock components.

PP calculates planned cost.

PP takes Work Center capacity requirements into account.

PP automatically creates Purchase Requirements for non-stock components.

The product is scheduled and produced.

PP produces a Completion Confirmation.

The cost of the order is settled.

QUALITY MANAGEMENT, PLANT MAINTENANCE, AND HUMAN RESOURCES MODULES

B

 Wait! Before you read this appendix, be sure you are familiar with the different kinds of SAP R/3 business documents explained in Lesson 22.

QUALITY MANAGEMENT

Quality Management covers the processes of inspection, and recording and analysis of inspection results.

The main documents used in QM include the Purchase Order, Production Order, Goods Receipt, and Inspection Lot.

 Reaching Quality Management You can get help on Quality Management by choosing Help, Help Library, Materials Management, and then scrolling down the list to Quality Management.

Inspection is closely tied in with quality management, and SAP R/3 utilizes three basic "inspection terms" in the QM module:

- **The Inspection Catalog**   This groups information about materials such as attributes, possible defects, defect causes, and so on. It is a hierarchical list, matching similar characteristics. There are various combinations of characteristics that may be useful at different companies.

- **The Inspection Plan**   This contains master inspection characteristics, inspection catalog data, and inspection methods.

 Master Inspection Characteristics   These could include such characteristics as weight, color, surface finish, and so on.

- **An Inspection Lot**   This can stand alone, or it can be created as part of an Inspection Plan (see Figure B.1). Inspection results are recorded only for inspections that are done with an Inspection Plan. If you want to record inspection results based on inspection characteristics, you need to assign an Inspection Plan.

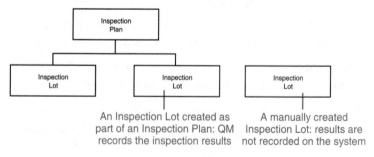

FIGURE B.1   An Inspection Lot can stand alone or be part of an Inspection Plan.

The following flow chart shows a typical sequence that illustrates what QM does. It's just one way QM could work at your plant. The setup at your plant could be different from this example.

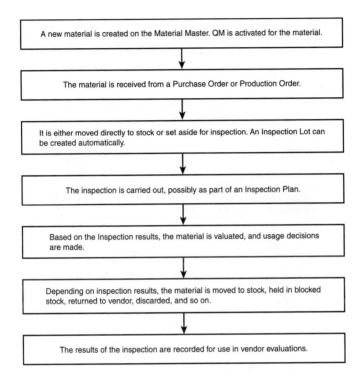

Quality Management can be set up (on the Material Master) in one of three ways: no quality management, quality management in procurement, or quality management with inspection processing.

QM provides many features to help you manage the quality of your goods:

- QM controls movement of goods in and out of inspection stock for both Procurement and Inspection Processing.

- With Procurement, you can block activity for quality reasons at several stages. Quotation, Purchase Order, and Goods Receipt can all be blocked. You can also block purchase of one material from a vendor, or all materials from a vendor.

- QM can also help you evaluate vendors, manage quality certificates, and set up Quality Assurance agreements and technical delivery terms.

- With Inspection Processing, QM controls Inspection Lot creation, sample drawing, recording of results, and usage decisions.

- Dynamic modification allows automatic adjustments of the sample sizes and inspection plans based on the quality level. For example, a recent lower quality performance would trigger more rigorous inspections.

- The Quality Management module is *ISO 9004 compliant,* including inspection planning, internal quality audits, quality system documentation, statistical sampling, test equipment, material traceability, and quality costs.

> **ISO 9004**   ISO 9004 is an international quality standard defining processes a company must use in order to be certified. Many buyers now require their vendors and suppliers to be ISO 9000 certified.

Plant Maintenance

The Plant Maintenance (PM) module helps you plan and control both preventative maintenance and repair of your production facilities and equipment. If your requirements vary from job to job (from planned retooling to emergency repairs, for example), you may use many of the tools in some cases and fewer in others.

> **Help with Plant Maintenance**   You can get help on Plant Maintenance by choosing Help, Help Library, Plant Maintenance. Be advised, however, that when the Help files refer to technical objects, they mean pieces of equipment or a plant location.

You must understand two key concepts to learn how the technical information about your plant is structured:

- **Functional Location**   This is the place in your process where equipment is installed. Two examples of Functional Locations shown in Figure B.2 are Number 2 Steam Plant Boiler Feedwater Pump and Number 2 Boiler Gas Burner.

- **Equipment**   This is a physical piece of machinery that was purchased on a certain date and has specific warranty information and a serial number. An example of this is the 500 HP GE 3 phase motor, serial #57200857, bought September 1989. (Equipment may be moved between similar Functional Locations, or may be kept in inventory as spare.)

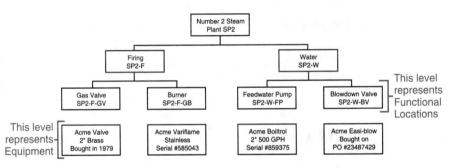

FIGURE B.2   A structure for Plant Maintenance.

This is one way the locations and equipment in your plant might be structured. Again, your plant may be set up differently.

The next flow chart shows a typical workflow for one way that PM could deal with an equipment breakdown.

Your workflow might be different depending on your plant and the urgency of the repair.

Some general PM information:

- The main documents necessary for PM are Maintenance Notification (which notes that something is broken) and Maintenance Order (which says "Go fix this").

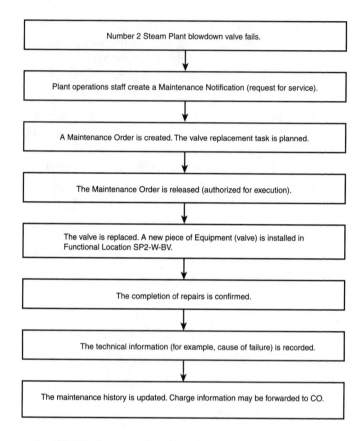

- The main master files involved are Functional Location and Equipment Master.

- PM can communicate to MM in order to take material from stock; it can also contact Human Resources for time keeping and Controlling for charge information.

- Using both Functional Location and Equipment helps you find causes for problems. For example, it can highlight if a particular functional location is a problem area, or if equipment from a certain vendor is giving you trouble.

- You can assign maintenance tasks to both internal and external groups.

HUMAN RESOURCES

Human Resources (HR) takes care of payroll, time recording, applicant administration, and organizational data. You can represent many different kinds of organizational structures in HR. Figure B.3 shows a sample company structure you could create in HR.

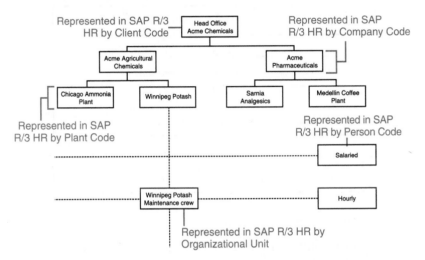

FIGURE B.3   One way of representing a company structure on SAP R/3.

There are many processes involved in HR and many activities related to organization and structure. Probably the most basic (and near and dear to our hearts) is payroll. The next flow chart shows a typical payroll sequence.

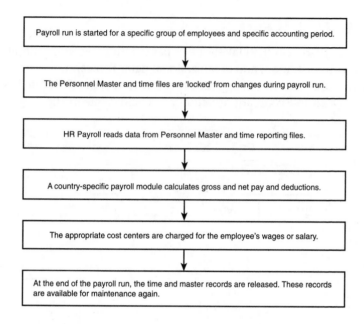

Some general functions of HR include:

- Tracking and controlling travel expenses and meeting room reservations.

- Accepting input from an external time recording system.

- Handling negative and positive time recording. In a negative time recording system, HR assumes the employee is working his or her scheduled shift, and subtracts any reported exceptions to this. In a positive time recording system, HR assumes that the employee works only the hours he or she specifically reports.

- Taking retroactive adjustments into account.

- Referencing holiday schedules for different employee groups.

- Using the Personnel Master File.

FINANCIAL ACCOUNTING, CONTROLLING, ASSET MANAGEMENT, AND PROJECT SYSTEM MODULES

FINANCIAL ACCOUNTING

Financial Accounting (FI) includes Accounts Payable, Accounts Receivable, Credit Management, Treasury, Financial Information System, General Ledger (G/L), and Extended G/L.

SAP R/3 Accounting Modules FI and Controlling (CO) are set up so that just one entry is required for each business transaction. There is no need to copy records from one subledger to another ledger.

The General Ledger provides a complete picture of all business transactions (see Figure C.1). It gets its data from automatic postings from subledgers. All G/L numbers are tied to source documents. So from the G/L level, you can zoom progressively to more detail until you get to the actual source document. The G/L collects all the accounts.

The following flow chart illustrates a typical workflow for selling a product and receiving payment, which is FI's primary role in the sale of a product.

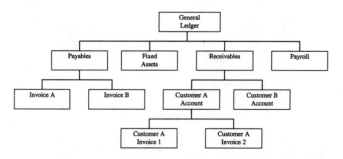

FIGURE C.1   One way a company structure could be set up in FI.

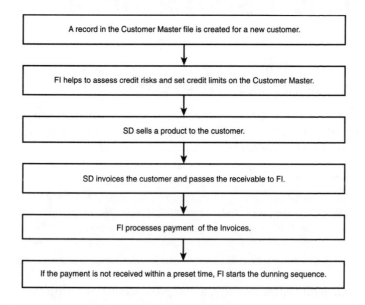

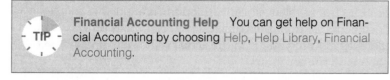

Financial Accounting Help   You can get help on Financial Accounting by choosing Help, Help Library, Financial Accounting.

Using SAP R/3's FI module is also beneficial for these reasons:

• Flexible closing reports are available for daily, monthly, and yearly periods.

- Non-SAP R/3 sources and destinations for data can be accommodated by using Automatic Procedures to batch data in or out. This allows you to interface SAP R/3 to existing systems in your organization where required.

- The Financial Information System helps you to evaluate customers and vendors.

- You can use Consolidation to aggregate the results from individual companies to a group of companies.

The main documents used in FI include Invoices (in and out), Credit notes, Payments, and G/L. The main master files used in FI are Vendor and Customer. FI interfaces to MM purchasing for Accounts Payable and to SD sales for Accounts Receivable.

CONTROLLING

In Controlling (CO), the cost accounting is carried out within a Controlling Area. This is not necessarily the same as FI, which presents accounts at a Company Code level. Figure C.2 shows a business setup for CO.

 Controlling Area A grouping that can be used to aggregate the control of several distinct companies.

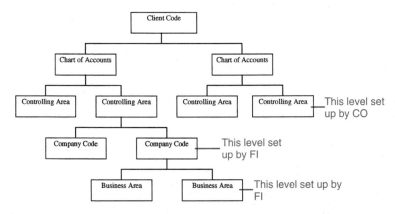

FIGURE C.2 One way a company structure could be set up in CO.

The following statements will help you better understand CO:

- A Controlling Area may contain one or more Company Codes.

- A Company Code represents a legal entity. A Business Area is a lower division and is used for internal accounting only.

- CO does Cost Center Accounting (CCA) and Profit Center Accounting (PCA). Costs are allocated to the appropriate accounts.

Controlling Help You can get help on Controlling by choosing Help, Help Library, Controlling.

To illustrate a typical flow in CO, we will look at how an organization could manage its telephone cost center to allocate telephone costs across cost centers.

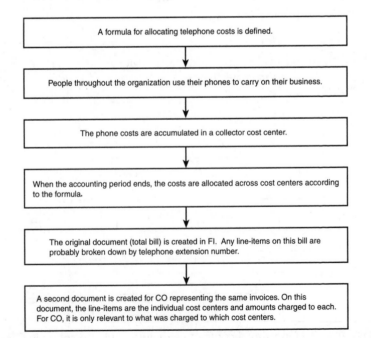

A formula for allocating telephone costs is defined.

People throughout the organization use their phones to carry on their business.

The phone costs are accumulated in a collector cost center.

When the accounting period ends, the costs are allocated across cost centers according to the formula.

The original document (total bill) is created in FI. Any line-items on this bill are probably broken down by telephone extension number.

A second document is created for CO representing the same invoices. On this document, the line-items are the individual cost centers and amounts charged to each. For CO, it is only relevant to what was charged to which cost centers.

CO also performs the following functions in SAP R/3:

- Tracks product costing and process costing

- Provides Profitability Analysis and Executive Information System

Executive Information System A system used to monitor key indicators that executives use to "take the pulse" of their business. The indicators chosen will vary from business to business. Facilities in which to look at the detailed data are usually also provided.

- Makes available both Periodic and on-demand reports

- Offers Business Planning and Control, Internal Orders, and Open Item Management

CO creates very little original documentation—it collects, groups, and charges source documents originating in other modules. The major documentation concepts used in CO are Cost Centers, Profit Centers, and Cost Elements. CO interfaces to General Ledger and the Asset Management module. Input is also drawn from FI and MM.

Asset Management

Asset Management (AM) provides tools to acquire, depreciate, evaluate, and retire assets. The kinds of assets covered are fixed, low value, leased, and real estate.

- Low value assets depreciate in the year they are bought and are often aggregated as a single asset master record.

- Depreciation often needs to be tracked (for more than one reason), so SAP R/3 allows you to depreciate the same piece of equipment in several parallel ways.

- SAP R/3 can represent company structure for AM in several ways. Charts of Depreciation can be at the same organizational level as Charts of Accounts, or depreciation can be a sublevel from Charts of Accounts (as shown in Figure C.3).

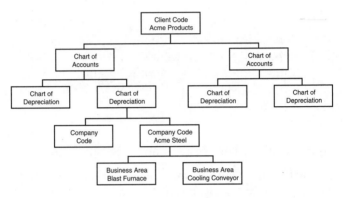

Figure C.3   One way a company structure could be set up in AM.

The next flow chart shows how AM manages an asset through its useful life (the asset's life-cycle).

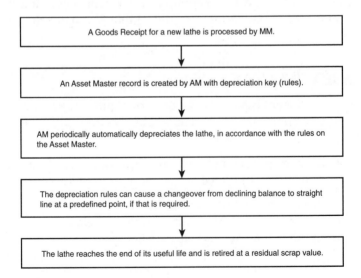

The main transactions used in AM are Acquisition, Capitalization, Transfer, Depreciation, and Retirement. The main master data includes Chart of Depreciation and Asset Master.

When an asset is acquired, it comes in through Materials Management. However, Asset Management can also transfer cost planning information to Controlling, and Asset Management can produce lists of ordered goods by location or room number to ease taking physical inventory or assets.

Project System

Project System (PS) helps you to plan, manage, control, and figure the costs of R&D projects, marketing projects, software projects, made-to-order products, and so on. The common tasks revolve around allocation of people, resources, and money within the framework of schedule and task relationships.

Accessing Project System   You can access Project System from two different menu paths; you can choose Logistics, Project Management or Accounting, Project Management. Go figure.

Help on Project System   In the help library, PS is part of CO. You can get help on Project System by choosing Help, Help Library, Controlling, and then scrolling down the list to Project System.

You break your project down into logical subdivisions and represent it in a Work Breakdown Structure (WBS). You can then divide the WBS by phases, assemblies, subsystems, or whatever makes sense for your specific project (see Figure C.4).

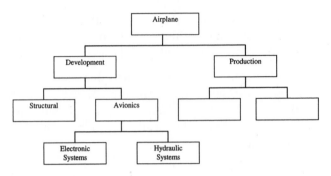

Figure C.4 A sample WBS for a new aircraft.

 The WBS This is a development step designed to assist you in working out task lists, relationships, costs, and so on. The WBS will evolve and become more detailed as your project progresses.

The flow chart shown here illustrates one way you could use PS to plan, execute, and control a project.

 Gantt Chart Lists tasks down the left-hand side, ordered by start date. The bottom of the chart lists the weeks or months. Horizontal bars represent the length of each task.

This list summarizes some of the advantages of using PS:

- Throughout the project phases, actual (as opposed to planned) costs and dates are fed back into the model. A Project Information System is available for tracking results to date. (You can also track project costing in a variety of ways.)

- You can use the SAP R/3 Documentation Management System to track project documentation (document owner, location, and so on).

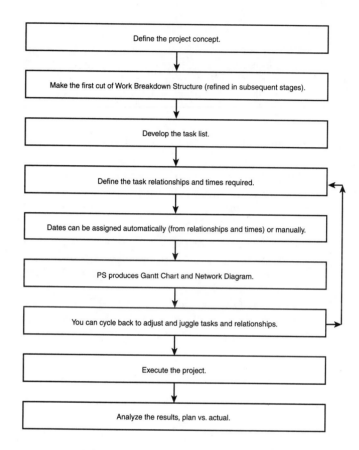

- Both capacity planning and cost planning are available in PS.

- Availability can be confirmed on Materials and on Production Resources and Tools.

- PS can control and track work assigned to outside resources.

- You can do *loop* analysis on your task networks with PS.

Loop   A sequence of tasks in which you can follow the prerequisites back and end up having a future task as a prerequisite for a past one. PS will help you exorcise these demons if they sneak into your project plan.

The main document elements involved in PS are the Work Breakdown Structure, Gantt Chart, Network Diagram, Activities (tasks), and Bill of Materials. When you use PS, you can make postings to CO, confirm materials through MM, and verify production resources and tools with PP.

Exchanging Project Data   You can exchange SAP R/3 project data with Microsoft Project using the .MPX format. If you are in the middle of a project and decide to change project management tools, you can move your data into the new environment.

INDEX